THE

BLUEPRINT

(A HANDBOOK FOR THE YOUNG BLACK
COMMUNITY MOVING FORWARD)

BY MIKAL A. WILLIAMS

Self-Published

Edited By: Avalon Scott

Williams, Mikal, 1994 – The Blueprint: A Handbook for Young Black America Moving Forward by Mikal A. Williams

ISBN 978-1-7340438-7-7

Printed in the USA

DEDICATION

To my brothers and sisters. May the sunrise & never set on us as a people again. For my God-daughter, Neveah Braxton. In loving memory of my brother Shai, may he rest in peace! To the future, the generations of my family that are being brought up and the ones not yet born.

You are my drive, everything I do is for you. To give you a better life than I could ever have, starting early and spanning even past your lifetimes. One day you will read this and know that I, your older brother, your uncle, your dad, your granddad, even your great-granddad is the reason for our family fortune & he loves you with every ounce of his being. Ase'

Table of Contents

Introduction

Part 2: The Keys

Chapter 8
Financial Freedom or Financial Slavery

Chapter 9
Balance: Assets vs. Liabilities

Chapter 10
Group Economics

Chapter 11
Using Credit, Spending Money, & Paying Off Debt

Chapter 12
Your First Car & House

Chapter 13
Business Structures

Chapter 14
Inclusion, Nepotism & Generational Wealth

Financial Tools

Figure Your Net Worth

Budgeting Sheet

Tax Brackets

Financial Dictionary

INTRODUCTION

For many years, I have been advising family and some friends from all over the country on life and finances. I realized that the lack of a blueprint existed in our homes and in our communities all around America. So this handbook is a means of me expanding my reach and teach more of my people at once.

Joining the Navy may have been the best thing to happen to me being from The Cooper Road in North Shreveport, Louisiana. Where I'm from is very small, some would call country, city. Even though the Navy wasn't for me, it took me around the world twice & showed me that there is way more to life than just little 'ol Shreveport. I love my city and I will make it better, but I couldn't have learned that there was better out there if I never left.

Now I feel inclined to, as best as I can, show to my brothers and sisters, who also come from impoverished places like I did, that there is more to life and that we can have it all! Enough people have made it out and kept the secrets for themselves. The old saying was, "The game is to be sold not told.", but they were trying to sell the game to people who couldn't afford the price. I believe we have to share the knowledge and spread the wealth, that way, everybody eats, B!

This won't be a book trying to point out who did what to us and why we are the way we are.

We've had enough of that and I am too tired of everyone pointing the finger at who caused all of our problems, with few people offering solutions. So, I'm here to teach and hopefully inspire my community to want and actually attain more in this lifetime.

Personally, I agree with Tupac when he said, "I think it's time we start making some changes. Let's change the way we eat, let's change the way we live, and let's change the way we treat each other. See the old way wasn't working, so it's on us to do what we gotta do to survive."

I have come to realize that too many of us learn from trial and error because no one left us a blueprint. My friend Ryan and I, when starting business ventures, always say how much easier everything would be if someone left us a blueprint. This is my earnest attempt at giving you exactly that, a blueprint. I have tried my best to make the business and financial parts of this book simple enough for our youth and young adults to be able to read and comprehend.

After reading this I want, no I NEED, you to apply this to your own lives, then pass it on to the generation after you, and so on. My hope is for this to be OUR blueprint going forward because, as of now, we are either too misinformed or simply uninformed on how every other community reaches great success and attains so much wealth. One of my favorite African proverbs says, "If you want to

go fast, go alone. If you want to go far, go together."
I want us all to go far, so let's go together!

PART 1: THE UNRAVELING

Chapter 1: Know Your History, Know Yourself

Most of us have no idea of our personal history, or as a race of people, but it is time to change that narrative. I suggest that everyone reading this does an ancestry kit for both of your parents' DNA, if possible, to learn more about your family and where you are from. If you feel the price is too high, you can split the cost between you and your siblings. There should be no excuses. If it were shoes, clothes, or a new game system you would find a way.

It seems we are still the only race who hasn't completely grasped the importance of knowing our history. As the late, great, James Baldwin said, "Know from whence you came. If you know from whence you came, there are no limitations to where you can go." The people who stripped us of our history, our heritage, even our last names understood how important it was. Any other race on this earth can pinpoint which country they are from, simply by their last name. They can learn of their ancestors' accomplishments directly, hence giving them a sense of real pride in their people. It also gives them an idea of the things they are capable of.

That reason is exactly why we need to learn our ancestry. That is why this may be the most important chapter in this book because we need to know what we are capable of. My brother, my sister, we aren't any of the horrible things that they portray us to be and our history DOES NOT begin with slavery! Nor is Egypt our ONLY place of greatness, for those who may know a little history. First off, we are literally the first people to walk this earth. This is a fact. It is scientifically proven because the oldest skull ever found was that of a black woman that they named, "Lucy".

It is proven that we civilized societies, yet they would have you believe that we were savages running in the wild with spears before slavery and/or colonization. A group of Africans called the Moors (mainly from the African country Morocco), went to Europe and showed them a multitude of things like mathematics, art, astronomy, and agriculture. We even taught them hygiene, how to bathe with soap and brush their teeth.

Their teachings were mainly in Spain and spread throughout Europe. To this day, in Spain during the festival of Moors and Christians, they have a parade called "Three Kings" to celebrate the Moors and everything they brought over their 700-year rule of Spain. It was known as Al-Andalus instead of Spain in those times.

Believe it or not, we were also the first to settle in the Americas. That's right. It has been proven that we were here first as well. Remember the oldest skull, Lucy. Well, the oldest skull ever found in the Americas was said to be Lucy's first cousin, meaning that it was also the skull of an African. It is proven that certain groups of Africans were sailing back and forth to America 300 years before Christopher Columbus got lost and landed here in 1492.

The Egyptians, the Moors, the Olmecs, all blacks, all those of African descent, were here well before Christopher Columbus. Some sources even say that we were settled here at least 60,000 years before any other group of people came to the Americas. Yes, that means we were here before the "Native Americans" as well.

The proof is all over, we just haven't been looking. Or, we've been looking in all the wrong places. In the USA, there are caves in southern Illinois with Egyptian hieroglyphs. There are objects covered with hieroglyphs in Cincinnati, Ohio as well. Then, if you look in Middle and South America there is evidence of Moorish civilizations as well as the Olmecs. The Olmec head statues date back to at least 900 B.C. and are found in places like Tres Zapotes (present-day Vera Cruz, Mexico), San Lorenzo (in Peru), and La Venta (present-day Tabasco, Mexico) all in Middle America.

Even though it is said that the Mayans were in Middle America before the Olmecs, they didn't rise to "greatness" until after they adopted most of their culture from the Olmecs. The Olmecs were excellent farmers, artists (first statues made in the region), mathematicians, and astronomers. For this reason, the Olmecs are referred to as the "Mother Culture" of Middle America.

Did you know that California was named after a Moorish Queen by the name of Calafia (or Califia)? The state was named by Spanish explorer Hernán Cortés and it is said that he had 300 black people with him on that exploration. Queen Calafia was said to have an army of strong, beautiful black, amazon like women. They were trained up for a battle against Christians who were defending Constantinople. Even though the Queen lost in the end, she inspired many.

While this isn't hidden, it isn't exactly taught either but there is a Disney movie, *Golden Dreams* where Whoopi Goldberg is depicted as the queen. The movie is about the history of California. There's a depiction of Queen Calafia on the 4th floor in the Senate Rules Committee Hearing Chamber in Sacramento called, "The Naming of California". There is also a seven-foot monument with her and her "amazons" at the Mark Hopkins hotel in San Francisco.

If you go back to Ancient Egypt, (Kemet) you will see that this is also were the world's first physician comes from after antiquity, his name was Imhotep. This is only a small portion of the greatness we have done throughout history. Now that we understand that we are more than America depicts us to be, or have convinced us that we are, it is time to return to glory!

They would have us believe that we have always been impoverished savages, but that is so far from the truth of our natural state that it hurts me to see how far we've fallen and that some of us don't seem to care. Did you know that the richest man in the history of the world was an African King in the country of Mali by the name of Mansa Musa? His wealth was literally too much to be quantified, meaning they couldn't put a number on it.

It is time to do better, to be better in the name of our ancestors. In the name of our children who will inherit this world after us, and their children after them. We are descendant from greatness. That means we are great, always have been, always will be!

CHAPTER 2: GET OUT OF "THE TRAP", THE GAME IS RIGGED

In this day and age, there is too much knowledge at our fingertips for us to be as misinformed and oblivious to the real world as we are. We can and must get the bigger picture to get as much as we can, while we can. But the world isn't set up for us to win, that's why there's so much 'hidden knowledge' out there. Some of that knowledge I will uncover in this book. But don't stop here, continue to seek more knowledge after reading this book for there is always more to learn and the game is always evolving.

The setup starts young, we are taught to go to school and get a good education so we can work for someone who never went to college themselves. That's because the game is all about leverage. Subconsciously, we know, but we leverage the wrong thing, our time! The poor and middle class wake up every day and leverage their time for money at someone else's job.

Money that we only use to pay bills and survive. You know, keep our heads above water. While the upper class is taught to leverage their money for time. Time to spend with family, time to spend pursuing their passions, to make more money, to make more time & prosper. So, if we can understand that, we must then put our unproductive ways aside.

With us being glued to social media, every day we see millionaires being made and get to see them enjoy the finer things in life, but we don't see the how. The grind. The sacrifices. Do you know what they did behind the scenes? All the partying, drinking, shopping, and constantly eating out that they had to give up in order to make those dreams a reality. Since we see these people shining, we want to shine too.

So, for us lower class people, when we get a little piece of change, we spend it on the finer things' which sets us back. Our minds tell us that we did what we should be doing, even though right after we buy that materialistic thing or take that "well deserved" vacation, we're right back to struggling! Is that one vacation better than a financially free life? Was it worth missing a payment or being late on a bill because you felt you needed a break? We say we do, but it's like we don't even realize that the cards are stacked against us in this game.

Like Tupac said, "We gotta get an understanding of the levels and the rules of the game. Once we get an understanding of what the levels and the rules of the game is, then the world ain't no trick no more, the world is just a game to be played." I am trying to teach us, but we have to be willing to learn and apply the information learned.

Quick scenario (all numbers are fictitious), let's say you had $1,000 and no bills due, would you rather:

A: spend $650 on a vacation to your dream destination and have $350 leftover?
B: Invest $1,000 and make an extra $350?

Most of us would choose "A", because we have this thing about instant gratification. When /we work, we want it to pay off NOW! But if we get away from instant gratification, we would see that "B" is the better choice.

It may take a little longer with "B", but the reward is greater. Let's say you choose "B" and invest $1,000. Then you get your $350 guaranteed. That is a 35% return on investment (unlikely in the real world, but again, just an example) which you could let compound. That means taking the initial money ($1,000) and the profit ($350) and reinvesting it.
So, now you have $1,350 with the same 35% return, which gives you $472.50 on to off the $1,350. That is a total of $1,822.50 and if you wanted to take that trip costing $650, you would come back with $1,172, instead of only $350.

I truly believe instant gratification is one of our biggest flaws when it comes to work and payoff. We have to learn how to play the long game and think of the big picture. If we invest smartly from the time we are out on our own, we'd truly be able to "live our best life" at all times and way sooner, instead of struggling and living check to check until we are old and gray.

It seems none of us plan to live that long with our "I could die tomorrow" and "You only live once" mentality. That type of thinking is why when we do die, our children have absolutely nothing! Not even the money to bury you with. How can you really say you love your family, then still leave them nothing but debt and struggle when you knew better? How could you, when you knew there was more? When are we going to put some actions behind our words?

Do we ever stop to think, why do they call it "the trap", or is it that we're too addicted to the lifestyle? None of us know who or where the term comes from or understand the meaning. But to me it is exactly what the name says, A TRAP! No one makes it out untouched. Well not many, but are the odds really in your favor?

You know almost all of your friends living the "street life" are being murdered, rotting in a cell, or barely escaping at least one of those two options on a daily basis, yet you go down the same road. Is it that you're too scared to do something different? I wish we could realize that if we put that street hustle we have into a legal business, we could easily make millions. Not just talk, rap, and dream about it!

We say we're woke, but our eyes are wide shut. I am directing this next question to anyone who may be reading this and is living the "street life". Have you ever stopped to ask where the drugs come from and how they get into the hood? We know cocaine isn't grown or produced in America. We know the average black person doesn't own planes or boats to get it over here. We know we aren't personally going to get it ourselves and bringing it back. It's time we connect the dots. Someone is pushing an agenda & we continue to play right into their hands.

I've seen so many military weapons in "our" hood that it's ridiculous and we don't own any manufacturing companies. So how does it all get here? Who brings it and why? I can promise you it's not for our health or protection; and I can promise you that it's not to give us a chance to make real money without actually putting in work. Remember what Tupac said in the song *Changes*, "First ship 'em dope and let them deal to brothers. Give 'em guns step back & watch 'em kill each other" That still holds true in 2019, but it's time out for it.

As I said earlier, I was raised in a neighborhood called the Cooper Road in North Shreveport, La. Now, I won't go into detail about it, but I had so many altercations with people when I was younger just because I was from "The Road". As a kid I never understood because I couldn't help where I was raised, but that didn't matter, I had to stand my ground. As I got older, I realized that we have pride over where we are from because it made us who we are.

My thing is, if we're going to have so much pride in our neighborhoods, why not own them? Why not buy a house on that street you claim? Why not get together and buy that corner store or gas station in the neighborhood, instead of it being ran by outsiders who don't care about anything besides stuffing their pockets? I can promise you that the feeling of ownership is better than just claiming it. One of my biggest goals, if no one from my neighborhood beats me to it, is to buy our neighborhood grocery store.

By owning that grocery store and running it better than the owners do now, more people from the area will shop there. More people would want to work there, in turn helping create revenue for me as the owner to put money back into the community via scholarships, etc. I want to play a big part in changing every aspect of my community, including our pattern of thought.

I see a lot of us who don't seem to care if we live or die. If you don't care about yourself, I can't change that, but what about your sons and daughters? Our little sisters and brothers who look up to us? Are we going to continue to abandon our kids? Our parents? If, & I do mean if, you're going to crash out, at least have a good life insurance policy and some money put away for when you die or get locked up and can no longer make that money that kept the household afloat.

That way, if you go, your child(ren) will be well taken care of. They don't deserve to be without either of their parents, but if you're going to live the street life, don't make them suffer for it and struggle too! Don't force your mother and the rest of the family to scrap together money selling plates & washing cars to bury you. There's nothing "real" or manly about that.

There's no real money in the streets anyway. Not enough to make you rich. If you're in the streets and you think you're going to be the one to beat the odds, remember what Nipsey Hussle said on *Overtime* from his Mailbox Money project, "You ain't gone get it 'til you see it right and jump off in this legal life, feel the pressure from your people right? But still choose to lead 'em right."

Actually, think about that second verse on *Loaded Bases* from his album *Victory Lap*. "I was sittin' on my Lincoln, I start thinkin'/ I ain't gone make 100 mil off in these streets and/ more than likely I'm gone end up in somebody's precinct/ or even worse/ a horse & carriage, front the church/ laid off in a hearse..." Again, only a small few make it out untouched, so get out while you can.

If your friends are really your friends, they will understand if you decide to change routes. They should be pushing you to do so. If not, are they really your friends? Is he really a friend or a snake in disguise, if he's giving you advice that will lead to your demise? It was different in the past. It didn't seem as if we had any other way to feed our families or to help mama with the bills. But today, there's too many ways to make a living and you don't need to go to college. Stop worrying about what people will say & how hard it will be at first. Don't be afraid to step out your comfort zone!

CHAPTER 3: AM I MY BROTHERS KEEPER? YES, I AM!

I'm sure we know the story of Cain and Abel from the bible, right? Cain killed Abel and when God asked him where his brother was, Cain replied, "I do not know, am I my brother's keeper?" I feel too many of our brothers and sisters have that same feeling towards each other when it shouldn't be the case.

We should all love each other as if we are actual brothers and sisters, but due to circumstances that I won't get into, we don't. This is one of our biggest downfalls and once we get this right, everything else should fall into place. Regardless of why we are this way, it is on us to fix it. This is a call to action!

We already know who did what and why they did it. I've had enough of us finger pointing and playing the blame game. That has gotten us nowhere, we have to make and take our own reparations. We have to start loving each other as actual family, once we get over that hump everything else will come easy.

Like Tupac said, "I got love for my brother, but we can never go nowhere unless we share with each other. We gotta start making changes, learn to see me as a brother instead of two distant strangers. And that's how it's supposed to be. How can the devil take a brother if he's close to me?"

It's a must that we love and respect each other. We have to get out of the mindset of respect being earned. Respect should be the given, disrespect should be earned only when someone has disrespected you first. Be your brother's keeper! Be your sister's keeper! That means not stabbing them in the back. That means not doing dirt against them. That means not bringing them harm, unless unavoidable. That means not pushing poison to them. That means checking them when you see them doing wrong and helping them fix themselves without bashing them or telling everybody their business.

If you know your friend has a significant other that is good for them, why let them do anything around you that would mess that up for them? If it was the other way around and you caught your friend's significant other cheating, they couldn't pay you not to say something. You wouldn't let them slip up like that if you actually cared. Don't be scared to check a real friend because as mad as they may be, they should appreciate it in the long run.

Once we begin to really love and look out for each other, a lot of the underhanded things in our community will go away. Let's say we treated the entire black community as actual family, answer these questions. Would you let your actual sister get beat on by her significant other? Would you let your actual sister or brother do drugs? Would you sell drugs to your actual sister or brother knowing the effects? Would you let your actual brother or sister get cheated on? Would you stand by and watch them slowly kill themselves with the unhealthy food that they eat? For some of these questions you might have thought, "That ain't my problem." But then you are no better than Cain.

Nevertheless, after answering these questions in your head, I believe you get the point. It's like what Brother Nuri Muhammad said in an interview, "The formula for black on black crime is simple but not easy. The knowledge of self produces love for self. Love for self causes you to do for yourself. You (the black man or black woman) are my other self. If I know me, love me, & am doing right by me & you are my other me, I'm going to treat you the same way."

See, we have lost the love we used to have for self, & it shows every day, even in things as simple as how we talk to each other. As Tupac said, "We went from brothers and sisters, to n***** and b*****." This loss of love, or self-hate has caused us to have this "crab in a barrel" mentality. Now, I am well aware that a crab's natural habitat isn't in a barrel and us black people aren't in our natural state either.

But where we are and how we got there are no longer the most pressing issues, at least they shouldn't be. We should be putting all of our efforts, time and energy towards getting to where we want to go, where we should be, where we actually once were, but you'll only know that if you've studied our true history. As I said earlier, we weren't just savages turned slaves, we were, and still are kings, queens, and gods, creators of our own lives!

I remember when Jay-Z first dropped his app *Tidal*. I know multiple black people who jokingly, or not, said, "I'm not buying that, he already got enough money. I'm not gone make him richer." But those same people pay $9.99+ a month for Apple Music or some other streaming service with multiple rich owners. Those same people will shop at Walmart, Target, etc. but won't support their friend or neighbor's business for fear of them succeeding and getting rich.

You would think they would rather see their friend get rich than to fatten some random person's pocket who could care less about you, your family, or your community. We have this idea that our brother's/sister's success means our demise, but this isn't slavery and that's not the case anymore.

I know you've heard it said a million times, I hope this time you overstand. You have the same 24 hours as that successful person has, and they print new money every day. Which means that there is more than enough for you and your neighbor to get rich and be successful. Actually, it would be easier and take less time for everyone to be successful if we all worked together to achieve goals.

CHAPTER 4: BREAKING GENERATIONAL CURSES

At this point, when we know exactly what our problems, our biggest struggles and issues are, we can't continue to blame anyone but ourselves. We know exactly what we need to do, we're just being too lazy to get up and do it. Why keep eating the same foods our parents and grandparents ate, when it is giving or has given them disease? Why keep relying on the same basic financial knowledge if we really want to prosper and give a better life to our community for generations to come? I'm sorry if I offend anyone, but we also can't keep waiting on someone to come out of the sky and save us, we have to save ourselves, first!

We can't be upset that our relationships aren't working like our parents and grandparents before us. We watched them function together while they were in a more stable place in life most times, while we young folks are still trying to get it together! You can't honestly expect a young man with no inheritance, no trust fund, or no passed down business from his family to be able to provide for you 100%, pay all the bills and have time for you at this stage in his life.

In all honesty, the ONLY reason men paid for everything in old days is because women couldn't work or weren't paid as much as men. Now, in a lot of cases, black women are more educated and have more opportunities than black men. Not to mention the high incarceration rate for black men. None of these to me are excuses, they are simply factors that we have to consider when dealing with our brothers. This is coming from a black man who plans to be the sole provider, but I have a greater understanding that it doesn't need to be that way. Anyway, just find what works best for your relationship.

Don't try to fit into this fairytale ideal mold, create your own. What works for you may not work for someone else because everyone's situation is different. Some black men may come from a little bit of money or have attained a little bit of wealth by the time you find him. In this case, he may be able to hold it down. But you can't expect that from a first-generation college student, barely able to afford college or any other man who basically comes from nothing and is truly trying to prosper. He would drown himself trying to keep you both afloat.

If you think a man should pay the bills then you have to grow with your man until he is able to do so. Again, we are still young and no one gave us a head start. Be patient with us, give us a little room for error. If you think it should be split 50/50, both the man and woman should be investing to make that saved money grow and work for them. However, in a lot of cases, the man has more "street knowledge" than the woman and maybe more experience. For that reason, the man should still be the head of the household.

Before you get offended, tell me what's wrong with letting a man, who actually has a plan, lead? I don't mean letting him be your boss and you bowing to him. I mean him actually having a dream for you as a couple, a plan to make that dream come to fruition and you following it. With that being said, men, make a plan and actually pursue it, show her you mean business and she will have no choice but to contribute to the greater good or get left behind!

In a lot of cases with men who actually want to provide, women don't know how to get out of their own way and let a man lead. It's almost as if some women would rather be in a relationship where they require more from their man than to be in a relationship where their man requires more from them. It seems as if it affects their ego or something. Almost as if having a man with more flaws than them allows them to get on him about his shortcomings so they don't have to work on their own.

My strong, independent women, we have to get away from these things when there's a real man present. It's great that you are strong, it's great that you can be independent, but with a real man in your life, you shouldn't have to prove your independence unless he's not around. If we could come together as man and woman and cut out all the games, then we could go to the Promised Land.

While I'm on the subject of man and woman, let me say that there is absolutely nothing wrong with getting to know multiple people at once when looking for a mate. The problem comes when you are sleeping with multiple people and treating multiple people like and/or telling them that they are the only one. Most of us see a problem with that because we are quick to have sex with a person after we see a few good qualities.

We should be taking the time to get to really know people and seeing the good and the bad. That way you don't waste your time in a relationship that will end up going nowhere or end up making a baby with someone you aren't capable of being civilized with. This would prevent a lot of wasted time and suffering by men, women, and children who have to deal with watching the two fight and only having one parent. "A child raised by one parent is unstable." - Nipsey Hussle.

Too many of us swear up and down that we are going to give our children what we've never had. We swear we're going to stop struggling one day, but we have the same habits as our parents before us who barely made ends meet our entire childhood. We don't really expect to go to work, pay bills, spend the extra money on materialistic things, repeat, then somehow stop struggling one day, do we? Albert Einstein's definition of insanity is doing the same thing over and over again while expecting the same results. We have to make a change!

Don't go out and party all the time and buy everything in sight because you have the money at the moment. Instead go invest the extra cash. If you have no knowledge then go learn or pay a professional. It's not as difficult as it may seem, just requires time and effort. We MUST also invest in a quality life insurance plan. $10k-$50k is NOT a lot of money in the grand scheme of things.

You should be trying to leave your child/family $100k or more and teach your family financial literacy. STOP LETTING YOUNG BLACK PEOPLE FIGURE OUT LIFE ON THEIR OWN! Also, own some property. Save up and put a down payment on a house so you know your children will have somewhere to stay when you are gone. Owning a home also adds to your net worth, while paying rent adds to someone else's.

When it comes to black business, we have to do better on both sides. We have to learn to support our brothers and sisters without asking for discounts and freebies all the time. We should be more comfortable with using our brother's or sister's service first, before stepping to someone else. Instead we only strongly support black owned business when a business owned by a different race has gravely disrespected and offended us as a people.

We should also understand that, as a whole, business ownership is fairly new to black folks, so please, be patient with us. With that being said, black business owners, we have to make our products and services, including customer service as quality as possible. As of now, professionalism and customer service are not our strong suit. We have to make it so that our brothers and sisters would WANT to choose us.

If only we treated all black businesses like we did black barber shops, we'd be on top! Barbershops have the most loyal customers & we literally won't get that service from anyone else but our specific barber. So why not treat all black businesses that way? We see the relationship it builds for the barber and for the client. Wouldn't you want that with anybody you shop with or sell to?

One of my friends made a Facebook post that said, "How long will we say f___ cancer and continue to put the things that cause cancer into our bodies." That question hit home for me as I know it is now for a lot of people who are reading this because we all have family or a close friend with or has died from some form of cancer. How long are we just going to continue to eat the easiest accessible food and wait until the next person we know gets cancer or diabetes and just accept it as "God's plan"?

Now, I am a vegan, but I'm not about to beat y'all over the head about not eating meat, y'all have heard that enough! What I am going to do is tell you that we have to add more fruit, vegetables, and herbs into our diets and DRINK MORE WATER. A huge problem I see is a lot of us don't drink water. People say it's nasty or they need flavor. Get some natural spring water and if you have it in your mind that you really need flavor, add some berries or any other fruit to give it taste. Certain fruits will even help detox and raise the pH level of the water.

Those fruit juices from concentrate aren't better, it has been found that the juice from concentrate causes cancer also. If you want juice it is best to make your own at home, but if not, get juices like 100% pressed apple juice. Even those aren't that good for you because of the pasteurizing, which is said to rob the fruit juice of its nutrients. We can no longer "live to eat" we have to learn to "eat to live" or we will continue to lose our loved ones way too soon.

Diabetes is big in our communities also and they would have you believe that certain diseases like that are hereditary and there's nothing you can do about it. That couldn't be further from the truth! You don't just wake up one day and have a bad heart because your dad had a bad heart. You get it from following the same diet your father followed and your body reacted the same way. In the words of Yada, "Disease isn't hereditary, bad eating habits are." Drink more water & do more exercises than just walking! It starts with us & I sincerely want us to do better.

Did you know that our stomachs are literally like a second brain, which is why people get "gut feelings" and a lot of times when we don't listen to those feelings, we regret it because our gut was right. Having a healthy stomach is key to having a healthy body and a healthy mind. Remember, exercise alone is never the answer. If that were true, people like Lance Armstrong, the professional racing cyclist, would never get cancer.

A lot of us have this crazy idea that just because a person lived up to 95 and ate whatever they wanted, that they did something right. It was luck of the draw. So, ask yourself this, that elder who lived to 90 or 100, were they healthy? Could they walk on their own? Were they still active? Could they breathe without oxygen masks?

Most of you probably answered no and I'm willing to bet that you will answer yes to at least one of these questions. Did they have diabetes? Did they have a hip or knee replacement/surgery? Did they have some form of cancer? Did they have a heart condition? A gall bladder problem? Most of the elders we know are living just to suffer; they aren't even enjoying life. We should be aiming for a good quality life in all aspects, not just a long one.

Maybe you'll get saved in the afterlife and that's cool, but in this lifetime, WE MUST SAVE OURSELVES! No one is coming down from the sky to do it. No one in office will do it. None of our parents or ancestors will do it, and the universe doesn't just magically make it happen. From our mental health, to physical health, to financial freedom. It's all on us. So let's take action while we're young to break this cycle and end "generational curses"!

CHAPTER 5: COGNITIVE DISSONANCE (OUR FEAR OF LETTING GO)

Before I get into this chapter, if you are a close-minded Christian, SKIP AHEAD TO CHAPTER 6! This chapter isn't for you. This one is strictly for those of us who are now or were ever curious about different aspects of Christianity or about the bible, but are too afraid to ask mama or big mama because we were all taught that "You ain't supposed to question God."

I don't want to run you off before you get all of the financial knowledge in part 2 of the book. So, again, skip ahead if you don't want to read my views along with some facts about Christianity. I think we should all read *The Historical Origin of Christianity* by Walter Williams so we can understand how this thing we call Christianity ever started.

Listen, I get it, we are so deeply rooted into religion, into Christianity, that to question it, is to question who we are. I mean it has been instilled in us from the time we were born. So, for us blacks, without a doubt, Christianity is as real as the air that we breathe.

After doing my research in the bible, I've come to know that nowhere in the bible does it say that we shouldn't question God. In fact, a lot of the people around Jesus (God in the flesh), actually questioned him. So why would they be able to question him, when they supposedly, saw him perform miracles in the physical form, while we never have? They were able to talk to him and get an actual response from a voice with a face. All we get is a voice in our head that somehow sounds just like us, but we believe it's him.

General Sara Suten Seti said, "Yeah I talked to God, then I woke my stupid a** up." He went on to say, "Yeah I talked to God, it was always when I was alone in the bathroom and when I felt like God was supposed to answer, I'd answer for him and say, Yes my son." I realized back in 2014 that I was doing the same thing and that's when I began to let go of Christianity. Not to say I don't believe in God or a higher power; I just believe differently than a Christian would. Sorry, I should've said I know better.

I know a lot of black folks are taught that we are the cursed people that the bible speaks of. I've always wondered, what did we do that's so bad that we are continuously raped in every sense of the word, oppressed, and killed off for well over a millennia? I have yet to receive a logical answer. The people I ask either dance around the question or get offended, but I honestly just want to know! See, before slavery in America, we were ruled by Arabs in Egypt for 1,200 years. What have we, as a people, done so wrong that the God of the bible would punish us for so long?

As a black man, knowing how important black women are to our struggle and our success as a people, why would I subscribe to a religion that tells me that black women are the reason for all sin on earth? Because we are the first people on earth, Adam and Eve would've had to be black.

Especially when our African spirituality like the Egyptians, the Yoruba, and more tell us our black women are of the highest importance in this lifetime. The foundation for Ancient Egyptian spirituality is Ma'at, an Egyptian Goddess depicted as a black woman, that stands for peace, justice, balance and truth. The goddess Nut, goddess of the sky; Hathor, goddess of love, all depicted as women of African descent.

Even the goddess, Isis, who is known as the "mother of god" for given birth to Horus and their story was taken in part to create the story of Jesus and Mary. Well, before the Europeans came into Egypt, the world's first "Holy Trinity" was Isis, Osiris, and Horus. They represented man, woman, and child because the two were married and had Horus and then we understood the importance of family. Even the story of the "Holy Ghost" was stolen from them because it was said that after Osiris was murdered, his ghost came to Isis and impregnated her with Horus. Sounds familiar right?

A lot of people who've never read their bible outside of church, and/or don't live by it in the slightest, are the ones I usually encounter. They are usually the most judgmental & defensive. Every knee shall bow, every tongue shall confess! Oh, I can't forget... "I am the way, the truth, and the life. No man cometh unto the Father, but by me."

Now, if we're real with ourselves we know it to be fact that there are civilizations that have been untouched by technology, colonization or any of those things. It is safe to say that there's both good and bad people in those lands, so why is it that those good people have to go to hell just because they weren't lucky enough to hear about Jesus and why was I so lucky to hear, especially when there's still no guarantee that I will go to heaven? Is one soul better than another? I don't think that's fair from such a just and righteous God.

We are told all the time, "Heaven isn't just for good people, hell isn't just for bad people." That's flawed already, but what drove it home for me was that when I research and learn about our African spiritual systems that we were a part of BEFORE Christianity, I learned that "Heaven" is for good people & "Hell" is for bad people. In Kemet (Ancient Egypt), there were three routes after death.

First your heart would be weighed against the feather of Ma'at, which represents truth, justice, harmony, and balance. Your heart will either be heavier or lighter depending on the deeds you did during your lifetime, whether good or bad. So, if you've lived a righteous life, gained as much knowledge as you could in your life, and have attained your highest spiritual awareness then you would be reunited with Amun (God) in A'aru or what we call heaven. Another route is reincarnation if you didn't gain enough knowledge or reach a high enough level of consciousness in your last lifetime. Then "Hell" meant that your soul could never be reincarnated, nor could your soul enter A'aru or Heaven.

Back to the topic, Ecclesiastes 3:11 says "He has made everything appropriate in its time. He has also set eternity in their heart, yet so that man will not find out the work which God has done from the beginning to the end." My question is, if we were never meant to find out what he did in the beginning & end, how do we have a book of Genesis & Revelation, which are the stories of the beginning & the end?

This made me feel as if someone is lying. Then if we go into Genesis and read the story of creation, it doesn't make sense. We know the Bible says it took God 6 days to create everything and on the 7th day, he rested.

Now, on the 1st day he said, "Let there be light." The confusing part there is that the Bible says he didn't make the sun, the moon, and the stars until the 4th day. So where was the light coming from for those first three days? Then, we have to consider that we are taught 1,000 years to us is one day to God. So, if it was a day in God's time, then there may have been 3,000 years where there was light shone on the earth without the sun, moon, or stars.

Remember, it says that the sun, moon, and stars weren't made until the 4th day (or fourth, thousand-year span). The story tells us that plants (fruits, vegetables, etc.) were made on the 3rd day (or three thousand-year span). Now, since the beginning of time, all plant life has needed sunlight to grow because the Creator designed it that way. So, how is it that the bible tells us that plants were made on the 3rd day but the sun wasn't made until the 4th?

One of the biggest problems I had is Isaiah 45:7, he says, "I form the light and create darkness; I make peace and create evil; I the Lord do all these things." How is it that he admits to creating evil (sin is evil), then sends us to hell for doing evil or sinning? Just doesn't fit the description of a "fair", "just", or "righteous" God.

Another thing that made me sick was, "God gives his toughest battles to his strongest warriors." It's like he kept trying to teach me the same lesson over and over when I already over-stood. Enough was enough! Forget me, why is it okay for little girls to get raped, for innocent people to get killed, or have their freedom stripped away, to be robbed of their land; their name; their culture, their entire identities?

My co-worker's infant son had open heart surgery, and thankfully, his son made it through. Obviously, that renewed his faith in God, but what about all the other parents whose sons and daughters didn't make it? Is it that my coworker prayed the "right" way and they didn't? God gets all the praise for the miracle. Well whose fault is it when the child doesn't make it? You're probably thinking, "My God wouldn't take no part in that." So, is it the doctor's? The devil's?

God made all things, right? God is all righteous, right? Then how could he create evil? Why would he create an angel that he, being all knowing, knew would turn against him and become the devil? Why would he create humans that he knew would sin, then send them to hell for sinning? Why send people to hell for not acknowledging you're their savior if they feel they've never been saved? These are just some of my thoughts being raised in a true southern, Baptist, Christian family.

I battled with this for a long time before I let go because as I said in the beginning, it was so deeply rooted in me. It was as much a part of me as my first and last name. To question that was to question who I am, and most of us can't fathom that.

Which is why when it comes to religion, even the "Christians" who hardly ever go to church, and/or don't live by the bible, get cognitive dissonance! If you're having too many doubts, but you're scared to detach yourself from religion, I'm telling you it is okay to let go! Find inner peace and believe in yourself first!

Better yet, why are we so afraid of looking into what our ancestors believed in? I think a lot of black people would feel more spiritually fulfilled looking into ancient African spiritual systems like Odinani, from the Igbo people in southern Nigeria, or the more commonly known Yoruba, or the Ancient Egyptians. If you've studied any of your history, you would know that most of the stories from Christianity were stolen from Africa in the first place. Which is why a lot of it resonates so deeply within us.

In part, we have been grossly lied to about our ancient practices. For example, the lie that Africans served and worshiped inanimate objects. The word Ase' (ah-shay), in Yoruba, is a word to acknowledge God in all things, that is why there is the common misconception that Africans worshiped trees or the sun. But don't let them fool you, we just appreciated ALL that the Creator gave us especially when it helped give us life.

Nonetheless, the word worship literally just means to honor or pay homage to something or someone. So, in a sense we did worship the tree for the oxygen that we breathe, and we did worship the sun because EVERY living thing on earth needs it to grow. But we didn't see them as actual gods. To reiterate, we knew that the Creator gave them to us so we simply appreciated what He gave us.

Due to years of study and research, it is now my wholehearted belief that, if it wasn't for outside influences, there would be NO Christians of African descent ANYWHERE ON THIS PLANET. It is a fact that we had no Christ or "Christianity" until Greeks and Romans came into Egypt and converted the Coptics, then the rest of Egypt and other parts of Africa, or until it was forced on West Africans by slavery.

Look into where you originated and see what they studied before slavery, before colonization, before Arab, Greek, or Roman rule or influence. Don't be afraid of what others may say because they themselves are most likely scared to seek the truth. God is in us all therefore we are gods, creators of our own experiences.

CHAPTER 6: THE LAW OF ATTRACTION: THE HIDDEN POWER OF YOUR SUBCONSCIOUS

Let me start of by saying that I know from personal experience that The Law of Attraction is a very real thing & it has been used in almost every religion and by the non-religious throughout history. Prayer, meditating, and/or manifesting, are all a part of The Law of Attraction. The law simply is that if you think good things, good will come to you.

If you in turn think badly, then bad things will come to you. See, your thoughts produce emotions and those thoughts and emotions are emitted into the universe. So, to stay on track with the law, always think of things that bring happy feelings and you will draw more positive things to you.

This law is one of the most 'slept on' Universal Laws of them all. But it is also one of the most powerful even when we don't know it, we are accidentally manifesting with this law. There is evidence all around us on a daily. A simple example is the Placebo Effect. People are given a pill with no nutritional value whatsoever, but they are told from a doctor that it can heal their affliction.

Now, just because the pill came from a doctor, they wholeheartedly believe, or think, that it will work. In majority of the cases, the placebo pill worked just as good, if not better, than the actual people. That alone should be enough to convince you of the mind's power.

Have you ever wondered why on certain mornings you wake up in a bad mood and you start telling yourself that it's going to be a bad day, then the day actually gets worse. Or, when you've already had a bad day then something small happens that pushes you over the edge.

Whether it be you stubbing your toe or dropping your keys when you're trying to get in the house. Ten times out of ten, you were constantly thinking about all of the bad that did happen, was going to happen, or could happen. Then that's exactly what the universe gave you.

As Nicki Daniels, owner of Shreveport clothing brand *Sleep Is For The Rich*, always says, "Your thoughts create life." From jobs, finance, your love life, to your health, it is all a manifestation of your subconscious mind. You may be thinking something like, "Well I didn't ask to get played or get my heart broken by my last ex, but it happened anyway."

That couldn't be more false. I'm willing to bet that before or during the relationship, you had negative thoughts about everything that could go wrong or what did go wrong in your past relationships. You thought about how all men or all women are the same and that's exactly what you manifested into your life, that same kind of mate.

That same negativity you don't want is all you thought about, so it is exactly what the universe gave you. See, the universe isn't listening to how you feel about the thing you think about the most, it's just going to give you what you're thinking about. So, if all you're thinking about is being in debt, you will forever remain in debt. But, if you start to think of being financially free instead, and act in that manner, the universe will begin to start to unfold that financially free life.

Oh, you thought you didn't have to take any action at all to manifest things. Well, even the bible will tell you that faith without works is dead. The opposite is true also, work without faith is dead. That is what people who feel they do everything right to have a better life don't understand. Most times, when their life doesn't match their hard work it's because they have a negative mindset. They put in the work, but they didn't truly believe that the work would pay off.

No matter what religion or spiritual practice you have, you can find evidence of the law. In Yoruba, it states that your Ori has to approve of the blessing that you are asking for, before "God" does. The Ori, in Yoruba, is your mind, both your spiritual and physical mind. This just means that nothing can happen in your life unless you truly believe, or should I say, unless you KNOW it can and will!

There are three simple steps to manifesting with the Law of Attraction. ASK, BELIEVE, RECEIVE. It's really that simple, but we've been so detached from our true selves that this may sound crazy and made up. There's hints about it everywhere, you just have to pay attention.

Have you ever wondered why certain things happen or pop up in your life when you can't stop thinking and feeling about them? Nipsey tried to tell us on multiple occasions, but I don't know if we were catching on. In the song. "That's How I Knew", from *Mailbox Money*, he said, "Rich n**** rules I believe in, manifesting gave me blessings, & that's how I knew..."

Now, think about it. Why do you think 1% of the world owns majority of its wealth? It's because they have taken our power, or should I say, they made us forget that we had it. You can literally have anything you want, just speak it into existence. For those of you who just started listening to Nipsey, I know you heard the song *Victory Lap* when he said, "This time around I'm gone make it clear, spoke some things into the universe and they appeared." He was literally talking about setting intentions and manifesting things into his life, all from the power of the mind. If the brain can conceive it, the body can achieve it, but you have to believe to receive it!

PART 2: THE KEYS

CHAPTER 7: SELF-DISCIPLINE & EMOTIONAL INTELLIGENCE

I saw this meme once that said, "You won't always be motivated so learn to be disciplined." I've never read anything more true. We all have things in this world that motivate us, but some days you lack that motivation. That may be due to life stressors or your own personal vices, but that's where self-discipline comes in and when you master self-discipline, nothing can stop you!

Be it discipline to get up every morning for the gym, discipline to go out and find that job you've been wanting after countless failed attempts that usually dampen your spirit, or too many other things. If life wasn't so hard, then the rewards wouldn't be so sweet! You just have to be willing to persevere.

Sometimes you lose all hope in what you're working for. Those are the days where self-discipline comes into play. For example, that person who's been eating right and working out faithfully but has yet to see desired results. The moment you feel like giving up, like it's all for nothing, is when you should push the hardest because if you can make it through those days, the other days will be a breeze.

On the other hand, if you let those days make you give up, you will backslide and regret it the moment you have hope again. In life, you will take losses. If you're an entrepreneur, you will take a million losses in your life, but this is where self-discipline comes in. That's when you have to get up anyway after you fell on your a** and keep it pushing.

I believe emotional intelligence is the key to self-discipline. Which in turn, is the key to self-mastery. In order to master ourselves, we must discipline ourselves. In order to discipline ourselves, we must take charge of our thoughts and emotions! I can't remember what that popular meme says, but it's something like, "If you make decisions off of emotions, you'll lose every time." Or like Dom Kennedy said, "You can't make no real decision based on emotion, and you 'sholl' can't make no money." So, it's a must that we learn how to control these things, because most times, this is our biggest problem and we don't even realize it.

For some reason, we think we have no control over our brain, so we let it run wild. I am a firm believer in the fact that we can't control initial thoughts and emotions, but we can control how long thoughts and emotions linger and what we do about them. We have to be conscious of our minds at all times. I am easily the most positive person I know, not because I never have any negative thoughts, but because I don't let them overrun my positivity or dictate my actions.

Once we understand that our thoughts truly do create life, then we will understand the value in controlling them, which will control our life. If all I do is think negative, then I will in turn do negative things, which will in turn make my life negative. But if a negative thought pops up in my head and I shut it down and replace it with positivity, when it's time for me to act, I act in a positive manner, which will have that positive impact over my everyday life.

The trick for me was, every time I thought negative, I made myself aware of it and replaced it with a positive thought. It took a while to do subconsciously, but that's exactly what ended up happening. I trained my subconscious mind to replace thoughts of fear and doubt with courage and hopefulness.

Now about these emotions. There's no way you can fully control how something makes you feel. But you can control how it makes you act or react. Those actions or reactions can in time change how certain things make you feel. Having emotional intelligence is key to success in relationships, business, and personal finance.

Think about how many times you or someone you know stayed with the wrong person just because of personal feelings for them or because of their "history" and ended up getting hurt worse in the long run. Or how many business opportunities people pass up every day out of fear of losing money.

How many times have we made unwise financial decisions like buying new shoes or clothes because we FELT like we needed that new shirt or those new shoes at that moment and regretted it later? That's all because we have no emotional intelligence, but if we really want to have a successful and prosperous life, whatever that means for you personally, then we have to take control of our thoughts and emotions.

We have this seemingly unconscious way of not taking accountability for our lives. The religious people give God all the credit for the good in their lives and blame the devil for all of their bad, but then what would you be responsible for? By that logic, you are just a puppet. Others point the blame to everything and everyone else for their success or especially downfalls. Everything in this life is in your control, from your thoughts, your moods, your weight, your quality of living, all of it!

Life doesn't just happen to you! When it comes to your thoughts and your mood, you can't fully control what you think, but you can control how long you keep the thoughts in your head and what you do with them. You can't control what someone does to you, but you can control how you react.

If someone cuts you off on the road, you'll most likely be mad about it for the next 30 minutes, or you may even let it ruin your day completely. Why though? I get that they ALMOST caused a wreck, but they didn't, and nothing about your life was changed. So why let it change your attitude? Let it go and move on with your day!

When I was in boot camp, a lot of us weren't in the best shape of our lives, but no matter how far behind you fell running laps you'd hear, "Never stop running." See the goal was to change your way of thinking. You know, mind over matter, and my RDC said something that will stick with me for the rest of my days. He said, "Continue to try until you die."

So, my message to you all today is to change your ways, never stop running! There will be hurdles in life, even potholes, but let none of it stop you. Even if you have to change direction, never change your final destination. Remember, the destination is more important than the route. "Before you run yo race, you gotta find the pace. Just make sure you cross the line and f*** the time it takes." -Nipsey Hussle

We are young right now, this is when we should be taking the most risks, failing the most, and going all out on ideas. This is not when we should be partying, clubbing, and vacationing every chance we get. Believe me, I love traveling. I've been around the world twice. But why not at least attempt to make it to where you can travel whenever you want, buy whatever you want, and do whatever you want?

If you have the entrepreneurial spirit like me, then take your risks, pursue that invention, start that business while you're young. Expect to fail! It is said that the most successful people have failed the most, so when you do fail, don't let it create fear. Learn from it and let it instead be fuel to your fire; let it drive you to greatness.

You have to understand that another person's success will never determine yours. So, if you see someone make it in the same line of work and you can't, you shouldn't envy them, but be inspired to do better, be better! Even if you see that a certain line of business has a high failure rate, who's to say you won't be the one to succeed? Don't let another person's failure stop you either! No matter what you've heard, your thoughts do create life!

Regardless of what you do in your life, no matter how hard you work, if you think negative then you will get negative results. Remember, this life is a marathon, not a sprint. It is all about endurance, who can last the longest! So, lace up, stay focused on that end goal, and never stop running!

CHAPTER 8: FINANCIAL FREEDOM OR FINANCIAL SLAVERY

There are four basic ways to make money in this society. As of today, most of us are only tapped into two sources. Author, amongst other things, Robert T. Kiyosaki calls this The Cashflow Quadrant. Well, this is my take on it for my people to understand or learn about it if they've never heard.

The quadrant should be looked at by side. The left side, I call "financial slavery". The right side, I call "financial freedom". On the left side of the quadrant you'll see E (employment) and S (self-employment) which I called, "Financial Slavery". On the right side you have B (business ownership) and I (investor) which I called "Financial Freedom".

Allow me to elaborate. Being an E (employee) is cool, stable (not really anymore), there's potential overtime, even though I don't get why we think it's great to lose more time for a quarter more an hour, and good medical and dental benefits sometimes, but not really. The stability of working for someone else is what gets us, because we are all terrified of financial uncertainty.

So, we often work dead end jobs knowing we could do better, but getting complacent and being fearful of the unknown keeps us working there for years or even a lifetime longer than we should. Being an employee is directly trading your time for a dollar. The moment you stop working, your money stops. In the E quadrant we are complete slaves to our jobs and usually to each paycheck. But people like me appreciate the worker bees, we need you for our business to thrive. Like they say, someone has to say, "Hi, welcome to Walmart".

Now, on the bottom left side, the S (self-employment) is the most appealing quadrant for those of us sick of the E (employee) quadrant, but this quadrant still requires exchanging your time for a dollar. Which to some of us is fine and it is actually my next step, but not my final one. But, as I suggested for you guys, I have already been working on the others.

For a lot of us in this quadrant, we love working hard manually and doing all the footwork for our businesses because it gives you sense of pride and freedom. In this way you are only kind of in charge of your financial liberty, but not completely because if you get sick one day and can't work, you miss a day of money, which could equate to hundreds or thousands of dollars.

This means little to no days or holidays off without losing money, depending on what your business offers to its customers. This is a good pit stop to financial freedom, but don't let it be your final destination. At some point, you should be looking to convert from self-employed to a full business with employees.

That way, if you still want to work in your business, you can still take days off without your business losing money. But remember, it is better to work ON your business than to work IN your business. Working in your business, you can get blindsided by your daily tasks and miss out on certain areas that need to be taken care of or possibly improved. Working on your business allows you to do just that, work on improving all aspects of your business.

Now, we are on the 'big boy' side of the quadrant. The side where we all should aim to be on before we are old and gray. The right side, the side I called "financial freedom". On this side we have the B (business owner) and I (investor) quadrants. These are the two that bring you, what Nipsey Hussle called, "Mailbox Money," which is residual income, money that comes to you whether you're sleep or working. This is where the wealthy live and we should be trying our best to move into this neighborhood.

In the top right is the B (business owner) quadrant, you own a business and may or may not be the CEO, but you have employees to do the work of the business. This can be very fulfilling. You make money without necessarily trading your time for a dollar and if you're smart, you might even bring in other people to be your CEO, or any other executive, in exchange for a part of ownership of the business. Now, our greedy minds will have us thinking, "Why would I give a piece of my business to a stranger when I worked so hard for it to be what it is?"

I'll tell you why with an example, at a point, Facebook was generating around $40 billion. Do you know how it got there? Because Mark Zuckerberg was smart enough to understand that he couldn't do it all by himself and even if he could, why not bring in experts who could do it 10x better than he could ever, which could potentially bring in 10x more profit? See, he would rather own a piece of a company generating $40 billion, than own all of a company generating $1 million. This can be a final destination because you have the freedom, but there's times where you WILL have to work if you are your company's CEO or any other executive. So, I guess it's up to you on this side of the quadrant.

For me, this ain't it! I am working very hard now because I am lazy and I want to, one day, never work again because I am a family man. I'd rather be grooming the next generation for the same amount of, if not more, success. So, to me, this is the pot of gold at the end of the rainbow. The bottom right is the I (investor) quadrant!

Let's be clear, you should start investing from the moment you get your first paycheck ever. Apps like *Robinhood* allow you to buy and sell stocks free of commission charge. For those who don't know, the commission is a fee you would have to pay each time you buy or sell any stock.

Now, all of that money you've earned and generated moving from quadrants E, to S, to B, should lead you here. Where you don't have to start or operate a business. Instead, you can invest in businesses for a percentage of the company or amass more wealth in real estate, etc. If all done smartly, you can sit back, go vacation, find a hobby, or whatever the h*ll you want to do. Watch your [smart] investments payoff and let the checks roll in without ever having to break a sweat. You can then truly live your life to the fullest!

If you're looking for somewhere to get started outside of buying stocks, I have a solution that can kill two birds with one stone. INVEST IN YOUR FRIENDS! How many of our friends have "million dollar ideas", or are starting businesses every day and don't have enough money, support, or other resources to start, or keep business afloat?

When your friend is going to file that new LLC, offer some money to help start up in exchange for a percentage of ownership of the company. This way, your friend gets the support they need and you now own piece of a company as a silent investor, which means you get a piece of the profits with little to no real risks, outside of the potential loss of your initial investment.

I hope this last Government shutdown was a wake-up call to us all that we shouldn't be so dependent on just one source for support. So many families were unable to eat or pay bills on time. They most likely had to turn to friends and family for support, or even had to take out loans etc., putting themselves into more debt.

All of this could have been avoided if they had enough insight, or had been taught not to depend on one source of income. Think about all of the families needing government support who couldn't get WIC or food stamps. They all suffered at some point in time during this shutdown.

This could all be prevented if we realize that one, the government should have little to do with our personal lives, especially our finances. And two, no matter where our income comes from, it shouldn't be the only source. I hope we get by now that there isn't much security in one job, not even a high paying one because people's lifestyle usually matches their job. So, one shut down, or you getting laid off, would flip your life upside down and simply saving won't make you rich either.

"How many millionaires do you know that became wealthy by 'investing' in savings accounts? I rest my case." -Robert G. Allen. So, we should all be aiming for at least two or three sources of income. To quote Robert Kiyosaki again, "It's not about how much money you make, but how much money you keep... how hard it works for you, and how many generations you keep it for."

CHAPTER 9: BALANCE (ASSETS VS. LIABILITIES)

They say old fools were once young fools and that is truly the case. If we don't go searching for answers or no one teaches us, we will forever lack knowledge. The saying is "You don't know what you don't know." So, I am hoping that my young black people will read, understand, learn from this book and actually apply it to their lives. This society is all about liabilities and assets. Finance, as well as life in general, requires balance.

Where we go wrong is, we spend our life acquiring so many liabilities and little to no assets. It's because we simply don't know any better. We are subliminally taught to buy what makes us feel or look good at the moment, with no regard for tomorrow. It's like we make $100 and spend $150. Which is why we continuously live check to check. It is why we live and die in debt. First, we HAVE to learn the differences in assets and liabilities.

A liability is anything you can buy that depreciates (drops in value) once you own it, and/or could cost you more money over time. An asset is anything you own that can appreciate (grows in value) over time and can make you money, or become a source of income. Today, we young people are controlled by liabilities. We HAVE to have the newest phones, whether it be the new $1000+ iPhone or the new $600+ Samsung Galaxy which both lose value as soon as you take it out of the box and you still have a bill to pay on it every month.

I see a lot of us buy a new car every time we come into more money (i.e. when income tax season comes), instead of paying off the one we have with that crazy high interest rate, just to get an undervalued trade-in, that we think is good, and a new, higher loan on a car that, you guessed it, loses value after you drive it off of the lot. If you're going to trade in a car, ever, make sure you have positive equity on the car. Meaning the trade-in value of the car is more than the amount you owe on the car.

Another liability, which is a hard pill for people to swallow, is student loans. No matter what dream they sell you, we don't NEED to go to college. There are millionaires made every day in this country with little to no schooling after high school. But, they would have you believe that the only way to make good money is to get a degree and ATTEMPT to work for a company who wouldn't care if you dropped dead. One of the biggest, self-made, black millionaires, Raynell "Supa Cent" Stewart, began her cosmetics line, The Crayon Case, with a GED and no college degree.

I said attempt, because people are struggling to find jobs in their degree field and end up working minimum wage jobs, still and living a lifetime of debt. Long term debt is, in almost all cases, a liability. I will explain the exception later. All the clothes, shoes, accessories are liabilities!

We HAVE to learn better, because if you knew better, you'd do better. While you may think of cash as the only asset, that is not at all the case. Owning a home is one of the biggest assets you can have, even if your home isn't paid off. The more equity your home earns, the bigger the asset. The equity grows with every payment made. The value of property minus the amount owed equals home equity ($210k market value - $150k left on home loan = $60k in equity).

Other forms of assets are commodities: stocks, bonds, annuities, IRA's, 401k's, mutual funds, and short term investments that we need to learn to get into instead of just putting our money into regular bank accounts. You could start with CD's (certificate of deposits) which are also assets because they grow, not only by the amount have you added each month of the CD term, but by higher interest rates than a normal savings account. If you must keep your money in a savings account, look for higher interest online bank accounts, not just the banks we see every day in our cities.

For example, most "good" savings accounts offer a 1.x% interest rate, but with a little research you can find multiple banks offering over 2% interest with low minimum balance and little to no annual fees. There's nothing wrong with buying "the finer things," just learn to have balance and know when you can really afford to do so. Aim for more assets than liabilities and you can truly "live your best life."

CHAPTER 10: GROUP ECONOMICS

This is something that our community has been unable to practice for far too long because of too many things. From greed, jealousy, hatred, you name it. It seems like we hate to see someone doing good, especially if they're doing better than us. As if their success means our failure, but that has never been the case.

I've seen people steal from their friend because they were being greedy. Not realizing that if they would have stayed loyal and tried to eat with their friend, instead of taking out of their friend's mouth, they could produce way more "food" and there would be more than enough for everybody involved. If only we would come together as a people, we could truly be great again.

Many communities practice group economics in their homes and in business, which is why they continue to flourish. Did you know that there is a Jewish birthright for them to travel to Israel when they turn a certain age, no matter where they are in the world?

This isn't government funded; it is funded by their own people. You know how that is possible? Group economics! Why shouldn't we have a birthright for blacks to be able to find out their ancestry and travel back to that part of Africa when they're of a certain age? It can indeed be done in time.

So, where do we start with group economics? We can start with our high school children who get their first jobs and know little to nothing about the real world (even though we should be teaching our children in their youth). Ask almost any young black adult today, when they turned 18, their mama most likely told them it was time for them to move out.

If not that, then when they got a job, she took most of their check telling them that they had to pay or get out of her house. This is a huge mistake on our parents and I hope we don't continue the trend. It has become so common to go out into the world lost and on your own that some young black adults get criticized if they receive help from their parents. The struggle has been overly glorified. I say overly because there are definitely some things you can learn from struggling, but every lesson learned doesn't have to be a hard one and why struggle when you don't have to?

I'm going to be the type of father that allows my kids to live in my house as long as they need to. As long as they are respectful, their priorities are right, and they are actually trying to get their life together, I see no problem. I know some of our parents really needed the money and that's why they "force" us to pay them, but it was ultimately on them to better themselves before they had us.

So as we grow older and begin to have families of our own, let's better prepare ourselves financially so that we don't continue this cycle of forcing our kids out into this world with nothing because we couldn't afford to take care of another grown person, even though that person is your child.

There's a mom with three kids. She and all three of her kids own their own businesses. Needless to say, they are all grown, but they all also stay in the same house. Since they still live with their mom, they don't pay full rent, they instead split the mortgage four ways. This is how they were able to build their savings and fund their own businesses. They all have credit scores well over 700 also.

Think to yourself, what was your credit score at 18? What about at 25?

Your credit score was probably low at 18 and since you had to leave home at 18, you were forced to get a car with high interest rate with payments you could hardly afford working a minimum wage job that you needed the car to get to everyday. You probably missed payments, which dropped your credit score more and now at 25, you are probably still trying to repair it.

Do you get it yet? The reason why this cycle needs to stop? It's hurting us! Now think about if you had, instead stayed home until you were 25 years old. You could save potentially two-thirds or at least half of all your income from 18 to 25 (that is if you were serious about your future) and worked on building your credit score before it ever got damaged. Then when you step out into the real world, you'd have a little cushion for minor setbacks as you try to figure it all out.

A lot of us have friends that we have to see every day. Why not move in with that friend. Instead of paying $800 rent for a one-bedroom apartment, why not pay $500 a piece for a two bedroom? Then the two of you could split all the bills 50/50 and possibly ride sharing if you work together or near each other. You can use all that extra money to build credit, start businesses, fund hobbies, or help out family. Group economics was once key in our communities and we need to bring it back.

Another part of group economics is community pots. These started resurfacing a few years ago and I saw a lot of people capitalizing on it, but just as many people doubted it. Be clear, this is something people of African descent have been doing for a long time. The difference now is we have no trust in each other, which needs to be restored. Think about if your family or your group of friends has a community pot.

First things first, these aren't meant to give participants more money than they put in and they aren't supposed to stop, ever. It is supposed to continue even onto the future generations. They are meant to be used as help for all, from all. Let's use my immediate family for this example, my mother has 6 children. Including her, let's say we put $100 a month into our pot for as long as we live. Every month it cycles $700 to one of us, so if there were ever any surprise responsibilities that come up, or an idea I wanted to pursue, I would have the money to pursue it.

What if my entire family, including everyone from grandma, to aunts and uncles, to all adult cousins over 18 contributed $100 every two weeks instead? For lack of exact numbers, let's just say that's 40 people. That's $4,000 every two weeks or $8,000 a month to cycle through to each head of household in the family.

Now, almost anytime there is an emergency you know you'll be covered because you have the pot, you wouldn't have to worry about loans for a lot of things, you can just wait on your household's turn to collect the pot. This could pay for a family business, shared family real estate, or investing in maturity bonds etc., to build wealth for the entire family. If not your entire family, find all the ones you know you can trust and build a brighter future together.

CHAPTER 11: USING CREDIT, SPENDING MONEY, & PAYING OFF DEBT

One thing I know is that we all need a better understanding of how credit works. First, allow me to tell you my story. I've never had any late payments on any debt and I thought that was all that mattered. At around 20, my credit score was at a 750 and I thought I could do no wrong.

After all, a lot of the people I knew had credit scores in the mid-500's. But, I couldn't have been more lost. I didn't know that multiple credit checks, co-signing, etc. could have a negative effect on my credit score. It was something I would soon learn the hard way and I want to prevent as many as I can from suffering the same fate. So, allow me to explain the different factors that affect your score.

Payment history, average age of credit, total accounts, and credit utilization are the key factors to good credit. It is also good to have a mix of credit accounts. Payment history accounts for 35 percent of your credit and is the biggest factor. The next biggest factor is your credit utilization or amounts owed vs amount available, which accounts for 30 percent.

Next, is the average age of credit, which accounts for 15% of your score. The average age is when your oldest account and newest accounts were opened divided by the total number of accounts. It is good to have multiple accounts in different forms (i.e credit cards, personal loans, auto loans, etc.). The mix of accounts, or the total number of accounts, and new credit accounts opened are 10% a piece equaling the final 20% of your score. So, don't go applying for, or opening, multiple accounts at once.

My advice is to start early! If you are a parent reading this then follow this next step for your kids today. If you are a younger reader, then inform your parent or older sibling who may not be aware. After you have raised your score and taken control of your credit, you can add your kid(s) or sibling(s) as authorized users to your card(s), that you keep in good standing, and only use that card for small purchases. This will give them a longer credit history and raise their credit score higher than most when they become 18-years old.

You could also do a Self Lender account or a secured credit card. A Self Lender account is basically you putting 'x' amount of money into an account each month and it reports to the bureaus as if you're paying off a loan, but in actuality at the end of the period you will have accumulated a savings (the monthly amount times 12) and a higher credit score.

The secured credit card allows you to put money, usually $200 minimum, into an account and use that amount as a line of credit. You're basically borrowing money from yourself, but if you miss a payment the company through which you get the card will take the money from your deposit. Though the simplest way, in my opinion, is adding them to your card. There's no extra work involved besides adding their name and social to your account.

Then every time you make a payment, it will show on their credit report as well. Please don't add them to your card if you're not financially responsible yet. A lot of us only know how to ruin a child's credit, or our parents ruined it at a young age. It's time to build it instead.

It is best to use as little as possible on credit cards because low credit utilization helps boost your credit. Usually, 10 percent or less, but not 0. If you must use more, try not to go above 30 percent for max benefits. This could help someone with no credit in as little as 6 months. As far as unsecured credit cards, which are the normal cards, the same is true. Aim to keep utilization at 10% or lower also.

If you're like me, you might feel the need to always pay off your cards the moment you have the funds to do so, there's a better way! Like I said, keep your credit usage at 10% or lower but not 0. What I mean by that is this, let's say you have a credit card with only a $500 limit, and you use $300 in between reporting periods. It is best that when you pay, you leave 10% or less of the $500 unpaid ($20-$50) at least until after the company reports to the bureaus. Bureaus like to see that you are using your credit, but not too much of it.

Another tip is to not use your credit cards for large purchases unless you'll have the funds to pay it off in the immediate future. Don't go buy a new 60" Ultra HD TV just because you have the credit limit to do so. If you do this, depending on your credit score, you end up paying for the TV twice over, or at least a time and a half because of the interest rate.

Remember, higher score, lower interest rates; lower score, higher interest rates. Another thing, if you feel you're done with a credit card, don't close the account. Leave it open and just don't use the card or cut it up. This is because multiple accounts are good for your credit in the long run. Also, let's say the card you want to stop using had been in use for five years or more. To close that account would wipe away five years of credit history from your score, which in turn would cause the score to drop.

Someone once said, "If I can't afford to buy something three times over, then I can't afford it." A lot more of us should live by that saying! We need to learn restraint when it comes to spending money and realize that we don't need to buy everything we want right when we want it, especially when we have bigger goals. I see and hear people say all the time they want to save 'x' amount of money by a certain date, but few actually take action.

What I never see them do is change their spending habits or find a way to make more money to reach that goal, I guess they feel it will just appear one day. In the beginning of becoming financially stable, we sometimes have to go without. Maybe even become a hermit. To be a hermit means less or no clubbing, drinking, clothes/jewelry shopping, or eating out, only basic necessities. No extra spending for any reason! You can save so much in a short time this way.

My hopes are that once you get your credit up to par, you save up and buy a house. Too many of us spend our lifetime paying for properties we'll never own. Why not buy a house and be able to pass it on, instead of renting and paying off someone else's mortgage and furnishing their dreams? Give your children/family a leg up, instead of continuing this cycle of struggling.

I see people get their taxes and feel like they're on top of the world and they could be, if they were smarter with the money. Instead of trading in and buying a new car every time you get your taxes, put a few thousand on paying off the car you already own, some credit cards, or a loan. Paying your rent in advance only sounds good, but it's better to pay off debt. If you could pay off your debt and save your income tax money for two years, you could easily put a down-payment on a home and pay all associated fees.

When it comes to paying off debt, we think as long as we are making the minimum monthly payments then we are good. But that mindset is what keeps us in debt longer than need be. Let's say you have a credit card, a car loan, and a personal loan. Instead of making the minimum payments on all three, make the minimum payments on the two with the lower interest rates while making larger than minimum payments on the loan with the highest interest rate.

This will get that loan paid off faster. Next, you take all of the money you were putting on the high interest account plus the minimum payment of the account with the second highest interest rate and pay that loan off faster.

Now you're down to one loan, you take the money used for all three and pay off that last loan faster than the term. This not only eliminates debt faster, it also raises your credit score higher than it would if you paid the loans off at the end of their term.

CHAPTER 12: YOUR FIRST CAR & HOUSE

First things first, don't try and buy the fanciest car you can find, it pays to look good and you literally have to pay the price! Start out with a moderate car. For instance, my first car was a 2006 Nissan Altima that I bought in 2014, which means it was 8 years old at the time.

My suggestion is to get a car that's no more than 7 years old that way you are eligible for GAP (Guaranteed Asset Protection). GAP insures that if something happens to your car (i.e. theft or totaled from wreck) that your loan will be paid off in full, despite whatever other money you may receive. It's also covered no matter who was at fault for the wreck.

Now that we've covered GAP, I need you all to understand that it IS NOT okay to be paying over $200 a month for a bucket. I was paying maybe $190 a month for my 2006 Nissan, and I've seen people with cars made in 2002 in 2017 and 2018, paying car notes over $300 with over 100k miles on the car. This usually happens because of poor credit. When you have poor credit, they may sell you that older car for $5,000 but you'll end up paying double after all the interest.

Stay away from "bad credit, no credit" car lots. They are not your friends. Your best bet is to save up and pay for one cash. Even if you have to ride the bus or catch rides with somebody until you save up, it's better for your personal finances. Don't worry about what anyone has to say, they will probably be struggling to pay their note starting out.

If you feel that you absolutely cannot wait to save up, then fix your credit and get financed through a bank. Most, if not all banks won't even give you the auto loan if the price is too unreasonable and they have to give you a fair interest rate based on your credit score, unlike those car lots with the "bad credit, no credit" signs who swear they have your best interest at heart. Once you have the car, please don't put off any maintenance that your car may need. Anything minor could easily turn major, don't ignore leaks, ticking, squeaking brakes, etc. and get oil changes regularly.

I bought my first house in 2018, a month before my 24th birthday. I said that, not to brag, but to let everyone reading this know that it can be done! I also feel inclined to share this information with my brothers and sisters. First, there are a few different types of loans you can get FHA, Fixed Rate, Adjustable Rate, Conventional, and VA for military.

There are a few others, but most first time home buyers won't be in the market for those. The type of buy varies also. You can buy new constructions, pre-existing homes, foreclosed/bank owned homes, or tax sale homes. Buying a home is a great business decision as paying off your home loan builds equity for you. As I said before, equity is the difference in what you owe on the mortgage from what the market value for your house is.

People often aren't prepared for the costs that come with buying a house outside of the mortgage. I'll share what I didn't know. When you apply for a home loan, you are allowed 14 days to shop around. Meaning you can apply for a home loan with multiple companies for 14 days and the inquiries won't hurt your credit, besides the first one of course.

Okay, so once you have been pre-approved for a loan the fun begins. You go house hunting and find the house you want, and you are ready to submit your offer. There are hidden fees you may not be ready for. After an offer is submitted and selected, you now enter the option period.

The option period is usually a full week (7 days) and you usually have to pay a $100 option fee, plus earnest or good faith money. Earnest or good faith money is exactly what the name says, money to show good faith that you are actually going to pursue buying the house that you submitted the offer on. No one wants their time wasted! That money is usually 1% of the cost of the house, so if you're buying a $200k house, the earnest money is usually $2k.

Sometimes you can get away with paying a little less maybe like $1.5k or $1k. Usually, to be turned in within three days of your offer being accepted. If the deal goes through, the earnest money will be added to your closing costs. During the option period is where you are allowed to pay for inspections etc. on the house. While home inspections are optional some loans require certain inspections (i.e. the VA requires a termite inspection to be done).

Regular home inspections are usually in the ballpark of $350+ and they are VERY thorough, inspecting everything from the roof, to the foundation, and everything in between. The termite inspection shouldn't cost more than $100 more depending on where you live. If the inspector finds any problems, you can have your Realtor submit your concerns to the seller to either fix them or give you, the buyer an allowance to fix.

You can also have the money deducted from the overall sales price of the house. If the house has termites, they must be treated immediately! During or after the option period, you will have to get the house appraised. The appraisal shows how much the home is worth, which could benefit you or hurt you in a sense.

If the house is appraised for less than the asking price from the seller, then you have two options. Either the seller must come down on the price or you will have to pay the difference out of pocket. That is if you really have your heart set on the house. Some programs, like the VA loan will not pay more than the appraised value. If the house is appraised for more than the asking price, then lucky you! Once you close on the house, you just got instant equity.

After all of that is taken care of, it is smooth sailing up until the closing date. The closing date is usually 25 days away from the day your offer is accepted. Until closing, you shouldn't apply for or open any new credit or touch the money you have set aside for closing costs. Closing costs are usually between 2% to 5% of the purchase price. Certain loans limit the amount of closing costs a buyer is able to pay, so make sure you pick which loan type fits your financial situation best.

That's a ton of money to be paid out of pocket, and you can't forget the down payment which is at least 3% of the sales price. Which brings me to my next thing. There is money out there, you just have to look for it. There are down-payment assistance groups and programs that will give you grants as a first-time home buyer.

A grant is money that you DO NOT have to pay back, not to be confused with a loan. There are also grants and programs that help pay closing costs in the form of a grant. Just do your research. As for your monthly payments, they consist of your principal and interest, homeowner's insurance, taxes, and in some cases, mortgage insurance.

For me, the VA loan was the best loan because there is no down-payment, a limit on what closing costs I was allowed to pay, and no mortgage insurance. A conventional loan is not insured by the government in anyway. The other FHA and VA loans, however, are government-backed.

An FHA is the most common, but requires you to make a down-payment of at least 3.5% and you will have mortgage insurance which will increase your monthly payments. Despite which loan you choose, you will have the choice of a fixed rate or adjustable rate. Fixed rate means your monthly principal and interest will be the same for the life of the loan.

Adjustable rate loans, usually called ARMs, means the interest rate will typically change every year after an initial period of time. There are different types of ARMS, which they call hybrid because they have a fixed rate for a certain amount of time, then they switch. There is a 7/1, 5/1, & a one year ARM, meaning a fixed rate for 7 years, 5 years or 1 year, then changing or "adjusting" the year following. I really want my people to pursue home ownership, there is so much pride in owning, especially when you can do it at a younger age. There should also be pride in being able to pass the home on to your children.

CHAPTER 13: BUSINESS STRUCTURES

I am a firm believer that everyone should have their own business. No matter if you want or have a secure job or not. For one, those "secure" job aren't as secure as they were back in the industrial age. You never know when the company will downsize, or shut down, and you get laid off. I don't believe any one thing or person should have complete control over my income, which takes me back to my first statement; EVERYONE SHOULD HAVE THEIR OWN BUSINESS!

Even if it's just a drop-shipping company that sells cellphone accessories (which was one of my first businesses by the way).If you want your own business, you have to understand the different business structures along with the pros and cons of each. Then decide which is best for you, not what your uncle who once had a business in the 80's tells you to do. You could have a sole proprietorship, a corporation, a limited liability company, or a partnership. Each one has different fees, tax laws and liabilities associated with each one and they all vary with each state.

A lot of our people are taught to get an LLC, (Limited Liability Company) if we do start a business, and don't even know why. We feel so happy when we spend our few hundred dollars to startup, when really, depending on what good or service their business offers, they could've done a

Sole Proprietorship and started sooner while also spending little to no money for filing fees.

Side note, an LLC may very well be the best option for you, but after reading this, you'll at least know why and you will know all your options. Also, just because you start a company as an LLC or whatever, doesn't mean you can't later change it to a different type of business. Although you will have to pay fees to do so.

A Sole Proprietorship just says I am Mike and I fix cars. So, my businesses name could be "Mike's Fix -N-A-Flash". The only filing I would have to do would be a D.B.A or "doing business as". Which literally means I'm Mike am I am doing business as "Mike's Fix-N-A-Flash". With a Sole Proprietorship, all money comes to the owner, which means the owner will get taxed as the business. This also means all liability falls on the owner, since he is not separate from the business.

Let's say Mike gets sued for improperly fixing the brakes, causing the customer to crash and be paralyzed. He will be financially responsible for whatever settlement agreed upon in court. Any cars, homes, or any other assets that Mike may own can be taken to settle the amount owed from the lawsuit.

Sounds terrible right? A sole proprietorship may be more suitable for a t-shirt company or something with little risks or hazards involved. Think of it this way, if your product or service is more on the expensive side then you may not want a sole proprietorship.

A better choice for small business is almost always an LLC, or limited liability company. Despite it being slightly more expensive to file for, the way you are taxed is better and there is less liability that falls on you as the person. If someone sues your business, you as the person wouldn't be financially responsible for it. It would come from your business.

Let's say you get sued for $10,000 and you only have $4,000 to your name. You would be in big trouble as a sole proprietor because you'd have to come up with that other $6,000. Now, if you own an LLC instead, you could use money from your business to pay off that $10,000 and never touch the $4,000 that you have personally. Even though it would usually cost more for an LLC, you are allowed to have business partners which means the fees can be split.

So, if you have two friends who want to go into business with you and the LLC costs $300 in your state, it would only be $100 per person. For obvious reasons, this is the best choice for first generation business owners like ourselves who never had any guidance or a blueprint laid in front of us. Let this book be your blueprint and let your business and lifestyle be the blueprint for your children, or any family members who'll inherit this world after you.

A partnership may be formed by two or more individuals, but may also be formed by two companies planning to work together for the foreseeable future. A general partnership is similar to a sole proprietorship, except there is more than one owner. So instead of Mike's Fix-N-A-Flash, it would be Mike and Mark's Fix-N-A-Flash. In this general partnership, both Mike and Mark own and operate the business. They both also share the profits, losses, and liabilities. Remember you only have to file your business if you want a D.B.A. (doing business as).

Now, a limited partnership must be registered as a business entity because one or more of the owners may just be investors or silent partners and have little to no say so in how the business is ran. For example, if Mark believed in his friend, Mike, but didn't have any knowledge when it comes to fixing cars. They could file a limited partnership where Mark invests in the business for a percentage of the company, which in return he gets an agreed upon percentage of the profits. This benefits both parties because Mike gets the revenue he needs to start, or keep the business running, and Mark gets to make a profit off of believing in his friend, without the possible liability besides the possibility of losing his initial investment.

Other than those two, there is also a limited liability partnership, which is like an LLC but none of the liabilities would fall on the partners, but solely on the business. Be mindful that most states only allow LLPs to certain types of businesses

There are two different types of corporations, C-Corporations and S-Corporations. But, honestly, C-Corps and S-Corps should be looked at when your business starts to grow large enough to where you need more legal protections, right now we are just getting started. Always stay up to date with different tax laws and reforms as they will affect each business entity differently.

CHAPTER 14: INCLUSION, NEPOTISM, & GENERATIONAL WEALTH

Derrick Grace II is on the money with his slogan "Family business or no business at all." Now, I know a lot of the older people had their crooked cousins or uncles come to mind and thought, "There is no way in h. e. double hockey sticks I would do business with them." You're right, those shouldn't be the family members that you do business with and those aren't the family members I had in mind either.

Almost all of our "business-minded" family members would have you believe that family members are the worst to do business with. If that is so, then why some of the richest people in modern times, are part of the richest families of modern times? You may only think of the Rothschild or Rockefeller families and think they were the exception. Let's not forget, the Walton family who are the owners of Walmart, the Quandt family, who are the owners of BMW, the Dumas family who own Hermes and many more.

There's no secret to how they do it, inclusion is a must. Not only inclusion, but nepotism. For my younger readers, nepotism is simply hiring family members at your business. A lot of the older readers may think, "Well I'm not allowed to hire family member at my job or even help them get hired because I would get fired." That's because that's your JOB, not your BUSINESS.

That same boss who told you that you'd be fired for hiring family, may very well hire his nephew for the position that you should have been promoted to. So, when you have your own business you could and should do the same. Inclusion is grooming a younger family member for the business by teaching them and taking them with you on calls etc. They can start learning early how the family business is operated. Then when they've grown and finished their education, you hire them and that is nepotism.

See, most of us aren't business-minded because our families aren't business-minded, which is why we see so many family members doing crooked business. We have to be taught while we are young, that nothing's more important than family and family business. A lot of people, not just family, are too greedy for their own good.

They'd rather steal or scam $100 from a family member, profiting $500 a month, instead of working with that family and potentially profiting $1,000 a month. Which means they'd make way more in the long run than the $100 they took that burned their bridge with that family member. As for me, I don't have any kids of my own, so I usually drop knowledge on my younger brother, sister, niece, and nephews.

I asked my nephew what was the most important thing in the world? He said he didn't know, and I told him that it's taking care of your family. No matter how much money he had, how many cars, or houses. It didn't matter if his family isn't straight.

I continued to explain to hi, the way to take care of family is, not by feeding them fish, but by taking them with you and teaching them how to fish as well. He didn't understand why so I told him, "If you go fishing and you come back and feed all of your family with your catch, there will be little to none left for you. But, if you take them with you and teach them how to fish as well, then there will be more than enough for the entire family."

That's where a lot of us go wrong coming from where we come from. We often try to feed everyone else while we're still trying catch enough fish for ourselves, and it leaves little to none. But, if we put our hustle and our mind power together, it would make more food and less work for the family as a whole.

If you feel like you must do it yourself, at least remember that you can't give away all of your bricks while trying to build your house. You have to finish building and then provide shelter for those in need.

But, when you think family business, it doesn't have to be aunts, uncles, and cousins if you don't feel they are trust worthy. It can be just you, your parents, your siblings, and your kids. Take them everywhere your business is involved. If you can't take them, tell them about exactly what happened, why it happened, and how it benefits the business.

Then, when you want to need break, want to retire, or inevitably pass away, you have heirs to keep the business rolling and to keep the money coming in as a family. Not some strangers, your blood whom you've groomed for this, who's entire livelihood will depend on it. Now, long after you're dead, the business that you created is providing for you family for generations after you're gone.

That alone is a great foundation for generational wealth because you left them a business and taught them the ropes. They don't have to worry about how to make a living. Their only focus in life should be how they will expand the wealth you left for the next generation after them and so on. Besides the business and the knowledge of the business, what else should you be leaving them? First off, more knowledge. Teach them about every single aspect of life, little by little, and make sure they understand to keep seeking more.

We should also be leaving them some real estate. Think of how much easier your child's life would be when they're an adult when they don't have to worry about where they will work or where they're going to lay their head. Imagine them chasing their dreams, while only paying property taxes, which are usually only a few hundred dollars a month, as opposed to them working for some company paying them minimum wage, and them trying to pay full rent. Think of how you struggle to do so, why would you want that for your child or children?

You shouldn't leave this world without owning at least one property for your successors. Then your children should all do the same, acquire at least one property in their lifetime, within a few generations, your family not only has the business that you started, but they are now in the real estate business, renting properties for income. As time continues, that's less and less manual work needed to be done to get paid, to live life in its purest form.

People love telling me "Money can't buy happiness." I will never understand why people even put money and happiness in the same sentence. There are happy, rich people and sad, rich people. There are happy, broke people and sad, broke people. One never determined the other, but you can never truly enjoy life if you're always worried about where your next dollar is coming from.

You can never truly find happiness being confined to someone else's schedule and plan for your life. Those same people who tell you money can't buy happiness, are the same ones who say money doesn't last forever. Well, tell that to the families that I named earlier. Some with six generations of millionaires and billionaires, working on seven. That could and should be all of us, so let's tap in with this blueprint and begin to create some generational wealth.

FINANCIAL TOOLS

FIGURE YOUR NET WORTH

ASSETS	
CASH	
CHECKING ACCT.	
SAVINGS ACCT.	
CERT. OF DEPOSIT (CD)	
STOCKS AND BONDS	
MUTUAL FUNDS	
401K/403B/TSP	
IRA/PENSIONS	
OTHER INVESTMENTS	
REAL ESTATE	
PERSONAL VALUABLES	
TOTAL ASSETS	

FIGURE YOUR NET WORTH (CONT.)

LIABILITIES	
CAR LOANS	
SIGNATURE LOANS	
BUSINESS LOANS	
CONSOLIDATION LOAN	
STUDENT LOANS	
CREDIT CARDS	
ADVANCES	
MORTGAGE	
TOTAL LIABILITIES	

Now, take your total assets and subtract the total liabilities to get your present net worth. Next, we will do a table to see what we need to achieve a desired net worth. Please be realistic.

DESIRED NET WORTH

TARGET ASSETS	
BASE INCOME (MAIN BUSINESS/JOB)	
2ND INCOME (PART-TIME BUSINESS/JOB)	
3RD INCOME (INVESTMENT/SIDE HUSTLES)	
ASSETS	
EQUITY	
TOTAL	

BUDGETING: CALCULATING MONTHLY EXPENSES

We must learn to stop living above our means and have better money management skills. The best way to start is to be aware of where all of your money goes. Let's stop the cycle of living paycheck to paycheck. Fill out the chart below.

EXPENSES	
MONEY EARNED	
GAS	
GROCERIES	
EATING OUT	
CLUB/BAR ADMISSION	
RENT/MORTGAGE	
CAR NOTE	
LOANS	
UTILITIES	
CAR INSURANCE	
PROPERTY INSURANCE	

If you get paid weekly, then break down monthly payments from your chart into weeks by dividing the amount by 4. If you are paid bi-weekly, then divide monthly expenses by 2. This way you can better understand how much of each of your check should be set aside for bills. As a young adult, you should have at least $1,000 in savings for emergencies.

Once you have your emergency fund, the next thing you should aim for with your extra income is investing. There are so many apps that are free to trade, and/or will teach you how to invest in stocks. My suggestion is that we all look for stocks that pay dividends. You won't get much back monthly/quarterly starting out. But think about if you were investing in dividends from the age of 18 to 30. You would have a steady stream of PASSIVE income at that age.

TAX BRACKETS

As our money, our income, our wealth grows, we have to be mindful that each "bracket" of yearly income we reach is taxed at a different rate. Though they are subject to change, here are the current tax brackets shown below:

Single	
$0.00 - $9,524.99	10%
$9,525.00 - $38,699.99	12%
$38,700.00 - $82,499.99	22%
$82,500.00 - $157,499.99	24%
$157,500.00 - $199,999.99	32%
$200,000.00 - $499,999.99	35%
$500,000.00+	37%

Head Of Household (Has Dependents)	
$0.00 - $13,599.99	10%
$13,600.00 - $51,799.99	12%
$51,800.00 - $82,499.99	22%
$82,500.00 - $157,499.99	24%
$157,500.00 - $199,999.99	32%
$200,000.00 - $499,999.99	35%
$500,000.00+	37%

Married Filing Separate	
$0.00 - $9,524.99	10%
$9,525.00 – $38,699.99	12%
$38,700.00 - $82,499.99	22%
$82,500.00 - $157,499.99	24%
$157,500.00 - $199,999.99	32%
$200,000 - $299,999.99	35%
$300,000+	37%

Married Filing Joint	
$0.00 - $19,049.99	10%
$19,050.00 - $77,399.99	12%
$77,400.00 - $164,999.99	22%
$165,000.00 – 314,999.99	24%
$315,000.00 - $399,999.99	32%
$400,000.00 - $599,999.99	35%
$600,000.00+	37%

Financial Dictionary

This dictionary will provide you with basic financial terms we should all be aware of. Some definitions below are simply for you to gain a basic understanding, please do more research when needed. Remember never stop learning.

# #

401(a) Plan – a retirement plan allows a percentage of your income or a dollar amount from you as the worker, from the company you work for, or from both you and the company. The money will sit and grow by interest rate in an account for a set amount of time or until you reach a certain age. At which point you can withdraw the matured amount through a lump-sum or annuity. Withdrawing before maturity age would result in penalties which means you would lose money for this and all other retirement plans.

You can also roll-over your funds into certain other eligible retirement funds etc. without penalty. This is usually offered by educational institutions, non-profits, and govt. agencies instead of by a corporation. A 401(a) is usually mandatory when working for one of the above-mentioned types of employers. The 401(a) is seen as a less risky plan vs. the 401(k) and gives the worker more control.

401(k) Plan - An employer-backed retirement plan that an eligible worker can make payments into from their salary before tax and is usually taxed when it is time to withdraw the monies at the time of retirement. This is usually offered by companies in the private sector.

A 401(k) is more so an option for an employee as opposed to the mandatory 401(a) so funds invested by the worker into a 401(k) may be matched by the company but this isn't as likely. The 401(k) has more investment options so it may often have more risk associated with it.

403(b) Plan – a retirement plan specifically for public schools and tax-exempt organizations. They may also be referred to as a "tax-sheltered annuity" A 403(b) is very similar to a 401(k) and investments can be either into an annuity or mutual fund.

408(k) Plan – a simplified version of a 401(k) that is set up by a company to help its workers save. Usually used by smaller companies with less than 25 employees. A self-employed person could also use a 408(k). The worker or self-employed person would invest pre-tax dollars into the account which would reduce their net income for the year meaning they'd save on taxes. (Ex. A person self-employed or working for a small company makes $40,000 and contributes $6,000 into the 408(k) for that year. When it is time to file taxes, the person would only be taxed on $36,000).

501(c) – for non-profit organizations. Organizations operating under 501(c) are exempt from paying federal income tax. There are around 29 different types of organizations under 501(c).

529 Plans – there are two main types of 529 plans, the 529 savings plan (qualified tuition plan) and the 529 prepaid tuition plan. The 529 savings plan can be used for children or adults. It is sponsored by educational institutions, states, or state agencies and may be used to cover the beneficiary's tuition, books, computers, room, and board. The money invested can go into equity, mutual funds, money market funds, ETF's and different protected bank products. In most of cases the earnings won't be taxed as long as it is used to pay only college expenses.

As far as the 529 prepaid tuition plan goes, you pay for credits at the college or university of your choosing to cover future tuition costs. These plans can't be used for room and board etc. The federal govt. doesn't guarantee prepaid plans and only certain states guarantee the money paid in. Each 529 plan varies by state. Also, there are fees associated with this plan that may lower returns. If you plan to use one of these for your child, the savings plan will most likely be the best bet for them to be able to focus solely on good grades and not worry about where any of their money for school will come from as it can cover all college fees usually without being taxed.

A

Adjusted Gross Income (AGI) – a calculation of income from your gross income to determine how much is taxable. Eligible tax deductions are taken into account beforehand to give you the AGI.

Advance – for my creators, whether it be music, inventions, artwork, or literary work, an advance is literally as it sounds. A company who "believes" in your work will pay you an upfront dollar amount to be able to use your talent and the work you produce but the catch is once your artwork, your book, your song starts making money, you don't get any of the royalties until that upfront dollar amount is paid back to the company.

So, let's say you get a record deal and they give you a $1M advance. Every dollar made from your music will go to paying back that $1M but what happens if your music doesn't do good enough numbers? That's right, you'd owe the remaining balance to the company out of your own pocket. So be careful when you are offered these advances for your work.

Annual Percentage Rate (APR) – the APR is how much interest you will pay each year on a loan until it is paid in full.

Annual Percentage Yield (APY) – usually applies to investments rather than loans. It is the annual interest rate if the principal and interest are left in the account to compound.

Annuity – a financial tool that pays fixed amount payments to the individual who owns the annuity. They are sold by financial companies who take your money and invest it over a period of time. Annuities are usually used by retirees but can be used by anyone especially if you have a lump sum of money that you want to turn into a steady stream. There are multiple types of annuities with different risks associated with them.

Appraisal – tells you the value of a property. Whether it be real estate, an antique, a collectible, or a business.

Asset – anything that you may own that will provide a future benefit. Anything that goes up in value or can generate cash flow.

B

Balance Sheet – a financial tool, like the one found in this book that helps a company or an individual figure their ass, liabilities. What you owe vs what you own.

Balloon Loan – any loan where you pay only a portion of the loan back throughout the life of the loan and you have to make one large balloon payment at the end to fully complete the loan repayment.

Balloon Payments – a large payment due at the end of a balloon loan. For example, let's say you take out a title loan for $2,000 over a six month period. For months one through five you'd be paying $250 which would pay $1250 of the loan back. The last month is when the balloon payment of $750 will be owed to complete the loan. This usually catches people off guard because they don't get enough info on the loan or they are in too much of a bind to care about it at the time.

Bank-Owned Properties – owned by a bank due to foreclosure etc. that may be able to be purchased at a lower price than what they are worth. This could benefit anyone looking to get into real estate with lower cost or someone looking for their first home.

Bankruptcy – when a person or company can't repay their accumulated debt. You, the debtor, would file a petition for bankruptcy at which point your assets would be looked at and may be used to pay back some of the debt. Bankruptcy gives you a "fresh start" while giving the company that you owed, some form of repayment.

There are 3 basic codes for bankruptcy under which you could file as a company or as an individual. There's Chapter 7, which would liquidate your non-exempt assets to pay your debt off. Chapter 11, which is more so for a business, deals with reorganizing your finances to be able to continue normal operation while making more money to pay back debt. Then there's Chapter 13, which you would still repay the debt yourself but owe a lower amount or be offered a lower monthly payment. With Chapter 13, you would be able to keep all of your assets unlike Chapter 7.

Be mindful that there are filing fees for bankruptcy and they vary by state. Also, not every type of debt can be wiped away by bankruptcy and filing for bankruptcy will also lower your credit score. A Chapter 7 stays on your credit report for 10 years and a Chapter 13 will stay for 7. Making it harder to get approved for any loans within that 7-10-year period or longer.

Barter – trading goods and/or services between two people without the exchange of money. For example, let's say you are a gardener and you need your grass cut. And you find a landscaper who is looking for the plants that you grow. Instead of you or the landscaper paying money, the landscaper would cut your grass and in exchange you would give him x amount of plants that would equate to the price of what the normal cost would be.

Bond – loaning money to the entity that gives you the bond with the promise of paying you back, usually with interest on the maturity date. Bonds have a coupon rate which could be looked at like an APR that would be added on to the initial value of the bond until the bond matures. So, if you have a $2,000 bond that matures in ten years with a two percent coupon rate, your bond would grow $40 a year for ten years. There is always a risk, whether small or big, of a bond being defaulted. To default means failure to repay you the principal and/or interest promised.

Bullion – gold, silver, or any other precious metal that is at least 99.5 percent pure. You can get these usually in the form of bars or coins. They are legal tenders, usually held by banks but people keep them as safety nets against economic crashes etc. For example, if America stops using the dollar system right now, what currency would you have? This is why people hold on to bars of gold and silver, it would be wise to do the same just in case.

C

Capital Gain – when you sell an asset for more than the price that you bought it for. After the sell, this gain must be claimed on taxes. There are certain exemptions for capital gains. For example, let's say you buy a house for $150,000 as a single person and the value raises to $200,000. You then sell the house for the full $200,000 that would be a capital gain of $50,000. Now, as long as you (the owner) lived in that house for two or more years, the capital gain would be exempt from taxes all the way up to $250,000.

Certificate of Deposit (CD) – a certificate with a fixed interest rate and a set date of maturity. Meaning you put in x amount of money and it sits and grows for an allotted amount of time. Understand that you can't touch the money invested until the CD fully matures unless you are willing to pay the penalty fees for early withdrawal. You can get a CD electronically through your bank and can choose to let it automatically renew.

Pay attention to the APR and APY when choosing your CD. The APR is the interest rate it will increase over the time you choose for your CD to mature. The APY is the would-be interest if the CD earns in a year. In my opinion. CD's just like every other investment are better when you let the money compound.

Charge-Off – when you have missed too many payments on a debt (usually six months of non-payment or not meeting the minimum required payments), like a credit card or a car loan and the company feels the debt will never be collected. This will NOT wipe the debt from your credit report. This will cause a big fall in your credit score and make it very hard to get any new credit accounts or loans. A charge-off will remain on your report for seven years.

Commerce – the exchange of goods and services between businesses or entities on a large scale.

Commodity – things like oil, natural gases, gold and other precious metals that can be used in commerce. Commodities can be bought for a certain price and sold when the price rises. For example, buying a 2.5g bar of gold when the bar is $200 and holding it in a safe or a safety deposit box until it's worth $300.

A lot of people believe we should hold onto commodities in cash the US Dollar becomes obsolete, meaning it would be completely worthless. In this case you would be able to use whatever commodities you have to acquire or pay for what you need.

Consolidate – to consolidate debt is to combine multiple accounts into one, which would cause a lower payment for you. For example, you have a $10,000 car with a $200 monthly payment. A personal loan of $2,000 with a $50 monthly payment and a home loan of $150,000 with a $1,300 monthly payment. That's $1,550 a month and a total of $162,000 in debt.

Now, if you consolidate it it won't erase any of the debt but the company in which you get the consolidation loan through would pay off all accounts then you repay them but with less interest in the long run and a lower monthly payment than the $1,550 you were paying before.

Copyright – makes it illegal for anybody besides the owner of an intellectual property to use it without the owner's consent. For my creators, be sure to have a copyright for your creations if they warrant it. If not file for a patent or a trademark & be mindful that they usually only last for a certain amount of time so be mindful of that & renew if you feel you need to.

Cosign – to agree to be legally responsible for a debt if the main borrower can't repay it. A cosigner is really only needed when one doesn't have good enough credit. BE CAREFUL with cosigning for people because a missed payment or two and now your credit is affected and you'll be partially responsible for repaying it. This could ruin relationships and slow your progress in life.

Credit Bureaus – there are three credit bureaus, Experian, Equifax, and TransUnion. All three valuate your credit history and give you a credit score. Your score will be determined using the FICO scoring system or the Vantage Score system.

D

Day Trading – when you buy stocks in bulk and wait for the price to go up, then sell them back for a profit before the end of that day. For example, buying 10,000 shares of a company and waiting until the share price goes up 2 cents. That would give you a $200 profit. Some people make their living strictly off of day trading.

Debt – money borrowed by a person or company from another. Debt is used to make purchases that you couldn't otherwise afford. It will always have to be paid back and with interest.

Debt To Income Ratio – how much money you make every month after taxes against how much debt you have to pay back monthly. Having a high debt to income ratio can stop you from getting approved for other loans.

Depreciation – when something loses value over time. Things like cars lose value the moment they are driven off of the car lot.

Dividend – when a company pays a part of its profit to the shareholders. Usually paid in cash and is paid out either monthly or quarterly.

E

Entrepreneur – a person who creates new businesses, taking on most of the risk and gets the majority of the profits. This creates more jobs for the economy.

Equity – what you owe on loan for an asset versus what the asset is worth. For example, if you bought a home for $250,000, in five years paid $50,000 of it off, and the value increases $40,000. Since the house would then be worth $290,000 and you only owe $200,000 on the loan. You now have $90,000 in equity, meaning that if you were to sell the house you would make a $90K profit. There are multiple other ways to use your equity without selling your asset.

Escrow – an account used to hold the payments from one party until the full payment requirement is met, then is transferred to the other party. For example, when you buy your home, all of your property taxes and home insurance will be paid into escrow. Once the amount for yearly premium for homeowner's insurance is met, it will be paid to the company through which you have the insurance.

The same is the case with property tax, it will be held until the end of the year and then paid to the county or parish where your home is. If you have an overage in your escrow account at that time, you will receive a check for the extra you paid. Beware, if there is a shortage, you will have to pay either at once or they will divide it up and add a monthly cost onto your mortgage until your escrow account has caught up.

Estate Planning – deciding how all of the wealth and assets you have acquired will be maintained and divided after you die. This can prevent dirty family members from trying to rob your rightful heirs of their inheritance but can also prevent your heirs from wasting all of the inheritance. This includes opening trusts, writing a will, setting up a power of attorney if needed, and adding/updating who will receive your life insurance benefit once you're gone.

ETF (Exchange Traded Fund) – collection of securities that trade just like stock. ETF's contain different types of investments like stocks, commodities, and/or bonds in an index, the prices move up and down as they are bought and sold until the market closes for the day. There's an Actively Managed ETF which exactly as it sounds, there will be someone making decisions on the portfolio.

This can cause the returns to not exactly match the ETF this could be beneficial or cause you to lose money. Simply put, more risk more reward but you will also have to pay fees to the broker managing your ETF. One of the major indexes that ETFs follow is the S&P 500.

ETN (Exchange Traded Note) – bond and trades like stock as well meaning the price will fluctuate. ETNs however, do not pay interest. So, when the ETN matures, the holder would be paid the return of the index it tracks. If the index is up $500 from when you purchased it, you will make $500 on top of your initial investment, minus the fees paid to the institution through which you buy the ETN.

F

FHA 203(k) Loan – for lower income families to be able to be able to purchase homes that badly needs to be fixed up. It would allow you to buy and renovate the house using the money from the loan. The loan would cover the price of the house plus the costs for labor and materials needed to fix the house.

Fiat (currency) – money that isn't backed by a commodity. For example, the US Dollar is a fiat currency because it is no longer backed by gold. The value of the American dollar is now based off of supply and demand and the stability of our government.

FICO Score – the first credit scoring model first created in 1956. This one was created by the Fair Isaac Corp. and is used to determine the risk of lending you money. I have noticed that a lot of times the FICO will be different from your Vantage score. Your FICO score will range from 300 to 850. Higher score means lower risk, so lower interest.

Forex (Foreign Exchange) Trading – exchanging one nation's money for another then trading back for a profit. When trading Forex, the currencies are shown in pairs like USD/JPY (US Dollar against the Japanese Yen) or USD/EUR (US Dollar against the Euro). The profit or loss is a result of the difference between the pair of currencies in which you trade.

The Forex market, unlike the stock market, is open 24 hours a day for 5 days a week. This is because we are trading around the world and obviously it wouldn't be adequate to trade when it is daytime on one hemisphere and night on the other.

G

Government Bond – issued by a government to support govt. spending. They can pay you in interest payments and are considered a low-risk investment because they are government-backed. There are multiple types of govt. bonds, not all of them pay interest.

Gross Income – the total amount of everything you make in a year to include wages, capital gains, dividends, alimony, interest income, royalties, rental income etc. before taxes or any other deductions.

Guaranteed Bond – a bond that promises that if the entity that gave you the bond can't pay you back the principal and interest that they owe you, it will be paid to you by a 3rd party.

H

Hard Inquiry (Hard Pull) – when a company requests your full credit report instead of simply checking your score. This will take a few points off of your credit. The hard inquiry will drop off of your report after two years and in turn raise your credit a few points.

Home Equity – the value of your home minus how much you owe on the mortgage for your home. If your home is worth \$200,000 and you owe

$150,000 you have $50,000 in home equity. Making larger down-payments and buying homes for cheaper than the market value gives you instant equity.

House Money Effect – when you as an investor or trader feels more comfortable taking a bigger risk on an investment because you are using money made as a profit instead of using your initially invested money (principal) or any other money earned from working.

When investing we have to be aware of our lax attitude when we make some profit to prevent this happen to us. This can hinder you from actually making profits and could cause you to lose the profit you already made and then some.

I

Indirect Tax – taxes paid to the government usually through retail purchases. For example, when you buy a 99-cent bag of chips and your total comes out to $1.09 that 10 cent tax collected by the store but is paid to the government.

Individual Retirement Accounts (IRA) – allows you to invest money to grow with interest until your retirement. Some employers offer to match contributions made to your IRA up to a certain amount or percentage each year. There are two common types of IRAs, a traditional IRA and a Roth IRA.

A traditional IRA allows you to deposit money that isn't taxed until you begin to withdraw it during your retirement. As for a Roth IRA, your money is taxed as you invest it but there will be no tax after it grows, and you withdraw it for retirement.

Investor – a person who puts money into something expecting to gain money in return. Whether it be paid in monthly or quarterly dividends from stocks, bonds, other funds, or royalties from a company they are part owners of.

Intellectual Property – things like trademarks, copyrights, and patents. They are legally protected from use or copy without proper consent from the person who owns the property.

Intentionally Defective Grantor Trust – with this type of trust that allows you as the grantor to pay income taxes on the trust over your lifetime so that the beneficiary doesn't have to. So, when you do go, there is no estate tax to be paid but after a set amount ($11,400,000 in 2019) the trust will be taxed at 40 percent.

Interest – broken down one of two ways, either simple or compound interest. Simple interest is a set rate on the principal or initial investment. Compound interest is a set rate on the principal and the incurring interest. Basically, the initial interest gained becomes part of the principal, higher principal equals higher returns with the same interest rate.

If you invest $1,000 and you make 4 percent in interest annually and you pull the money made on interest every year, that would on be $50 each year. But if you let the interest compound the first year you would make the $50 but the next year, your principal becomes $1050 and you make $52.50 in interest, year three the principal becomes 1,102.50 and 55.12 and so on.

J

Junk Bond – also known as a high-yield bond is a bond with a higher risk of defaulting. Higher risk also means higher possible returns hence the name.

K

Key Currency – currencies stable enough to be used in international trade and commerce. The seven key currencies are the US Dollar, the Swiss Franc, the Euro, the British Pound, the Japanese Yen, the Mexican Peso, and the Canadian Dollar.

L

L-Bond – when a life insurance policy holder needs money and sells their policy second hand if they are in need of money or can't afford the monthly premium. You as the investor, if you choose to buy the policy, would also have to pay the premium. When the original policy holder dies, you would receive a payout.

Lien – as a guarantee that repayment will be made on a loan. If the debt is not repaid in full, the company or bank which holds the lien will regain possession and ownership of the asset.

Lien Sale – public auctions on things like real estate, automobiles, and other personal property (i.e jewelry, collectibles, etc). You can buy delinquent tax liens on homes, and the owner has a specific amount of time to redeem the property from you.

Life Annuity – an insurance policy that pays a set amount to the owner (usually monthly) up until the policy owner's death. Usually used to provide income after a person retires.

M

Maturity Date – where an investment is fully grown and may be renewed or will come to an end. For example, if you have a six month Certificate of Deposit (CD), upon the day that marks the 6th month, you can renew the CD or withdraw your money.

Money Market Fund – a type of mutual fund that invests in different types of securities and has a short maturity date, usually less than 13 months. They are considered to be a low-risk, short-term investment.

Mortgage Bond – a bond backed by a mortgage or a group of mortgages. If this kind of bond defaults, the bond owners have some claim to the property or properties within the bond and can sell it/them off to make up for the default. Mortgage bonds usually have a lower rate of return than other bonds but are more secure, meaning lower risk.

Municipal Bond – issued by a parish, county, state, or municipal to finance its capital expenses (i.e. schools, bridges, and highways). They are exempt from federal taxes and a lot of state/local taxes.

Mutual Fund – made up of money from a group of investors that is managed by a professional and invested into different securities to make capital gains or income for the investors.

N

Negative Equity – when the value of your asset is lower than the amount you owe on the loan for your asset. For example, if you have $190,000 left on a mortgage and the value of your home is only $175,000, you have $15,000 of negative equity. This also applies to cars when you owe more than the market value or trade-in value of the car.

Nest Egg – a saved amount of money for a specific reason, like buying a house or expecting to be out of work for a set amount of time with little to no money coming in. Having a nest egg allows you to be able to live your normal life while in-between jobs.

If you are switching careers or quitting a job without having a second one lined up, you should always have a nest egg of savings for you to live comfortably for at 6 months. Side note, we need to get out of the habit of just quitting a job without another job already lined up.

O

One Percent Rule – for those of us who want to get into owning rental properties. The one percent rule gives you an ESTIMATED aim for how much you should charge for rent to make a profit monthly or at the very least, break even. For a $150,000 loan, you should be looking for a monthly mortgage payment of no more than $1,500. So then, you should charge a tenant no less than $1,500 for rent.

Opportunity Costs – the benefits you miss out on when taking one opportunity over another. This helps you make an educated decision on which opportunity to take.

Outsourcing – paying an outside source to do things that would've usually been done by you or someone else in your company to cut costs.

Overhead – all fixed, recurring business expenses like rent, insurance, any leases (on equipment) and utilities.

P

Paradigm Shift – a major shift in thought process, concept, and practice. A shift is currently taking place, be a part of it or get shifted. It will happen place with or without you.

Passive Income – what Nipsey called, "mailbox money" is money from rental properties, partnerships or owning a percentage of a company while actively involved in the company (a silent investor), interest from investments, and dividends. Passive income is taxed differently than regular income.

Patent – an intellectual property granted by the US Patent and Trademark Office (USPTO) to exclusive rights to a process, design, or invention for a set amount of time. So, patents have to be renewed to keep exclusivity. Although it may take a while to get your patent approved, once you are patent pending, anyone who infringes upon your property can be sued.

Perpetual Bond – a bond with no maturity date and can't be redeemed, meaning you can never get back your principal. On the plus side, it pays you a steady stream of interest payments forever.

Personal Trust – a trust that makes you, the creator of the trust, as the beneficiary.

Pledge Fund – a fund where all of the investors contribute a set amount of money over time to reach an investment goal. For example, a startup company looking to raise $200,000. Investors would contribute until they reach the goal and the startup company would offer different incentives depending on how much money each person/entity invests.

Ponzi Scheme – an investment scam promising high returns with low risks. They make money by gaining more investors and using their money as returns for the first investors. These schemes fail when there stops being any new investors. Please beware to not fall into a ponzi scheme.

Poverty – now we all know what poverty is, so I just wanted to point out that for a family of four (2 parents and 2 children under 18), poverty is a little $25,000. Basically if we stop acquiring so much unnecessary debt early on, we would be able to live better, sooner. $25,000 doesn't sound like much when you have a high interest car note, rent, high interest credit cards, etc. on top of normal bills but when we begin to set our kids up for success (i.e. getting them started early with credit and/or buying their first car), they will be able to thrive, even with their entry level jobs.

P/E Ratio (price-to-earnings ratio) – is formula that measures a company's share price to its earnings per share. A higher P/E ratio means investors expect a higher share price in the future. The formula is market value per share, divided by earnings per share.

Principal – on a loan is the original amount borrowed, with an investment, it is the original amount invested, or the face value of a bond, all before any interest is incurred.

Pyramid Scheme – a scam set up based on network marketing. Just like a ponzi scheme, you will be offered high returns and the newer investors' money is used as returns for the earlier investors. Usually you would be invited to a seminar by a friend who was tricked into it as well. At the seminar usually some wealthy, or seemingly wealthy person will talk and get you excited about joining the company. It isn't until you're inspired and all in when they ask for their "small fee" of, let's say, $500.

Now you've paid and are signed up, your next step is to get three of your friends to sign up under you so you can level up as a member. Now as they sign up and recruit more people under their name, it builds you up but notice how I haven't mentioned anyone making money or sales. That's because there usually isn't any actual product or service to sell and the only way to make money is if you stay in long enough to sucker enough people into joining like you. If it sounds too good to be true, it probably is.

R

Recession Proof – assets or businesses that aren't drastically affected in a negative way, due to recession. Assets like cash, US treasury bonds, gold and other precious metals are considered recession proof.

REIT ETF – an ETF that has most of its assets in REITs (real estate investment trusts). A REIT is a company that owns and usually operates with income producing real estate (i.e. warehouses, hotels, and apartment complexes). This type of ETF has above average dividends that can provide consistent income. REITs have the ability to survive in crisis if managed correctly because the properties owned will still generate income.

Revenue Bond – a type of municipal bond that will be used to build an income producing structure like a stadium or toll bridge. This kind of bond generally matures in 20 to 30 years. Usually sold at $5,000 per bond.

Rollover IRA – allows you to transfer the assets from a previous employer-backed retirement fund into a traditional IRA to keep the assets in a tax-deferred status and prevent the penalty of early withdrawal. An indirect rollover gives you 60 days to invest the money into an eligible plan but 20% will held by the IRS until you file your taxes for the year. A direct rollover is done by your employer so no funds will be held.

Royalties – payments from a company made to you as a legal owner for the use of your asset, property, or intellectual property.

Rule of 69/7072 – how long it will take for your investment to double with compound interest. You divide 69, 70, or 72 by your interest rate and that will give you a good estimate on how many years it will take. If you had an investment with a 7% interest rate, divide 70 by 7 and that tells you it will take an estimated 10 years for your investment to double. Using 69 is said to be more accurate when dealing with constant compounding and 72 is said to be more accurate when the compounding is less frequent. 70 is used more often because people feel it is easier to remember.

S

Secured Bond – a bond that is backed by an asset, if the bond becomes default, the asset's title will be transferred over to your name.

Secured Credit Card – as mentioned earlier in the book, a secured credit card requires you to make a deposit and that deposit will be used as a backup if you can't pay the balance on the card. Remember, the amount of money you deposit will be your credit limit on the card. Besides that, they function just like a regular credit card.

Security – a financial tool that holds monetary value.

See Through Trust – a trust that allows you to pass on your retirement benefits from your IRA on to a beneficiary after you are dead.

Silent Partner – someone whose only involvement in the company is providing capital. A silent investor would have nothing to do with the daily operations and have little to no say so in how the company is ran. The only liability you have as a silent partner is losing the money you invested if the company fails before a profit is made.

Soft Inquiry (Soft Pull) – when you, a potential employer, or financial institution you already do business with checks your credit. Soft pulls don't affect your credit score.

T

Tax Deed Sales – gives you full ownership of a home after you've paid the taxes and the owner doesn't redeem it in time by repaying you for the taxes plus interest. Tax deeds are sold at an auction and the highest bidder wins, but you only have 48 to 72 hours to pay the amount or the sale is canceled. The minimum bid will be the amount of the delinquent taxes, so if your winning bid is anything higher, that extra money will go to the previous owner if they never redeem the property.

For example, if your winning bid was $15,000 and the delinquent taxes were only $4,000, the previous owner would receive $11,000 because the government only cares to get what it is owed. But as the winner and new owner, you have instant equity from the value of the home and no lien or mortgage on it.

Tax Lien Certificate – when a property has unpaid taxes for the year (and has been in default for a certain period of time), a lien is placed on it and that lien certificate is sold at an auction. Buying the certificate means that you pay off the taxes for the owner. At the auction, you bid on the interest rate you are willing to receive, whoever bids the lowest, wins.

Once you have bought the certificate, the owner usually has 1 to 3 years to repay the amount of the taxes plus the interest agreed upon at the auction, usually ranging from 8 to more than 30 percent. Tax lien certificates have a much higher rate of return than other investments. On the flip side, if the owner doesn't pay you back in that one to three years, the property will become yours, but this rarely happens since there is so much time to repay you.

The Wealth Effect – says that people spend more as they make more money or gain an increase in value of assets they own. Beware of letting this happen to you because it could cause you to continue living check to check and one missed check away from struggling.

Title Loan – a loan that uses your car's title as the collateral in case you don't repay the loan. I had to touch on this kind of loan simply to tell you to beware! I've seen too many friends and family members falling into the title loan trap. When you are in financial trouble, a title loan will be very appealing because they don't usually run your credit and the process is fairly simple. The catch is they come with super high interest rates, which means it's harder to pay back the loan, which also means they would be able to immediately repossess your car.

Trademark – a word, phrase, symbol, or insignia that indicates a specific product to separate it from other products of its kind. For example, we all use facial tissues and almost all of us call them

"Kleenex" but that is a certain brand of facial tissues that has been trademarked and we would never see another company use that name because they would be sued.

Treasury Note – basically a debt to you from the government with a set interest rate. Treasury notes can be bought with a competitive or noncompetitive bid. Competitive meaning you can bid at the auction for an interest rate, noncompetitive meaning you take whatever interest rate is offered. The maturity rate on Treasury notes is usually one to ten years. With treasury notes, you will receive interest payments every six months until it matures, and you only pay federal taxes with money earned from them.

Trust – gives an entity (the trustee) the right to hold your (the trustor or grantor) property for a third party (the beneficiary), usually a child, grandchild, or younger sibling. There are multiple types of trusts. A bare trust is a trust where the beneficiary has full rights to the capital, the assets, and all income made from those assets within the trust (when they are 18 or older). There are living trusts and testamentary trusts. A living trust is as it says, the trust will go into play while you are still alive. The testamentary trust is for after you are gone.

An irrevocable trust is one where the terms cannot be changed unless agreed to by the would-be beneficiary, which is the one who will be receiving inheritance from the trust. With that being said, a revocable trust can be changed or canceled without the beneficiaries and the assets in the trust aren't transferred over until the death of the grantor, who is the person who made the trust.

U

Utilitarianism – "the greatest good for the greatest amount of people." We need to adopt this mindset when it comes to our community and begin to do what is best for us as a whole instead of having an "I'm gone get mine by any means, forget everybody else" mindset.

V

VA Loan – as I touched on briefly earlier, a VA loan is for anyone who is in the military for at least 90 consecutive days on active duty. If you're out of the military already, you must have served 24 consecutive months and not have a dishonorable discharge. There are a few other conditions, but these are the basic ones.

The benefits for the VA loan compared to other home loans is that there is no required down-payment, you don't have to pay monthly mortgage insurance, there is a limit on what fees you can pay for closing, and you don't need as high of a credit score for a good interest rate on your home loan.

Vantage Score – The second credit scoring model. The first version of the Vantage Score system was made in 2006 by the three credit bureaus. The Vantage Score is a combination of the three credit scores, as opposed to the FICO which breaks your score down by each bureau. It used to have a different credit range but adopted the 300-850 range with the Vantage Score 3.0 in 2013.

W

Wealth – the market value of all of your assets after you subtract all of your debt. So to be wealthy, like I said earlier in this book, have more assets than liabilities.

Weekend Effect – when buying stock, you will notice that the price and return is usually much lower on a Monday than the Friday before. You should keep this in mind when tracking a stock that you are considering buying, this can save you money and in turn make you more money when/if the price of the stock increases after you purchase it.

Will – a legal document that tells how your property and assets should be handled and who should get custody of your minor children.

Y

Yield –   measures the income (interest or dividends) that an investment earns over a period of time, usually annually, and shown in percentage.

FINAL THOUGHTS AND
ACKNOWLEDGMENTS

Remember that all the financial knowledge and tips in this book, no matter how advanced they seem to some, are just basic financial knowledge that a lot of wealthy people teach their children starting from their youth. I said that again to say, we must never stop learning. Learning shouldn't stop when you get out of school and it definitely shouldn't be the only place you learn. There is always more to know, and the world is ever-changing.

Fear nothing in your youth. Take risks, educated risks, to better your future. Don't be attached to anything material objects. Don't be afraid to lose money while betting on yourself. You can get it all back and then some. Think before you act and don't make a split-second decision that can ruin your whole life. Don't let fear make you end up living with regret for the things you could've done or should've done to make your future better for you and your family.

This book was written with nothing but love for my brothers and sisters, and I truly hope I have given you some of the basic tools to change your life and the lives of your families, forever. I quoted this African proverb earlier, but I need us all to really grasp this concept. "If you want to go fast, go alone. If you want to go far, go together." I really want us to go far as a people, so let's go together.

I want to thank all the people who helped make this book come into existence, either directly or indirectly. First, a thank you to the Creator, the Most High. A special thank you to my ancestors who have passed down this mindset that I have had since my youth and my early wisdom gained from them. To my editor and friend, Avalon Scott, for the guidance with this whole process. To my family for always having the utmost faith in me. To my friend, my brother, and business partner Ryan Braxton and his wife, Raven for the continued support, motivation, and inspirational words. Last, but definitely not least, the biggest thank you to my wonderful mother, who did the best she could and helped mold me into the man and the hustler that I am today. We have so many teachers right in front of our eyes, all we have to do is open them. Nipsey was teaching us with his moves as well as his music, but you have others who taught and still teach through lectures and/or through their demonstrations.

We have Brother Polight, David Banner, Derrick Grace II, Yada, Brother Red Pill, Brother Blue Pill, 19 Keys, Pop Darby, KT the Arch Degree, even some of your conscious friends, and more who are literally out here showing us better every day. You can find them on almost every social media platform, whether it be Facebook, Instagram or YouTube. They come from where we come from, look how we look, and they are acquiring, or have already acquired, exactly what we say we want out of life. Then you have master teachers like Dr. Phil Valentine, Queen Afua, Ivan Van Sertima, Dr. Sebi,

Frances Cress Welsing, Professor James Small, Min. Louis Farrakhan, Yosef Ben Jochannon, Jacob Carruthers, Dr. Amos Wilson, Dick Gregory, the list goes on & on, who have been teaching us the way for decades.

This is not to say I agree with everything these teachers say, but they all have one important thing in common, they are all for the betterment of our people. Please, if you don't know the works and teachings of anyone I named, research them, study them, apply the information, and pass all of the knowledge down. Let this blueprint help shift the paradigm. Finally, a special thank you to every individual reader. Ase'